D1554854

A Compendium of Bunk
or
How To Spot a Con Artist

A Compendium of Bunk

——— or ————————————

How To Spot a Con Artist

A HANDBOOK FOR FRAUD INVESTIGATORS, BANKERS AND OTHER CUSTODIANS OF THE PUBLIC TRUST

By

MARY CAREY

and

GEORGE SHERMAN

CHARLES C THOMAS • PUBLISHER
Springfield • *Illinois* • *U.S.A.*

Published and Distributed Throughout the World by
CHARLES C THOMAS ● PUBLISHER
Bannerstone House
301-327 East Lawrence Avenue, Springfield, Illinois, U.S.A.

© *1976, by* CHARLES C THOMAS ● PUBLISHER
ISBN 0-398-03498-2 (cloth)
ISBN 0-398-03501-6 (paper)
Library of Congress Catalog Card Number: 75-23221

With THOMAS BOOKS *careful attention is given to all details of manufacturing and design. It is the Publisher's desire to present books that are satisfactory as to their physical qualities and artistic possibilities and appropriate for their particular use.* THOMAS BOOKS *will be true to those laws of quality that assure a good name and good will.*

Printed in the United States of America
R-1

Library of Congress Cataloging in Publication Data

Carey, Mary.
   A compendium of bunk.

   1. Fraud.   2. Fraud investigation.   I. Sherman,
George, joint author.   II. Title.
HV6691.C37   364.1'63   75-23221
ISBN 0-398-03498-2
ISBN 0-398-03501-6 pbk.

This book is dedicated to
Marlene Kassin,
without whose help loads
of things would never get finished.

PREFACE

WHEN the authors began work on this book, they thought of bunco, or fraud, mainly as the concern of the police officer who is responsible for the investigation of the professional criminal — the dyed in the wool confidence man who delights in living by his wits. Two years and many interviews later, it has become apparent that fraud should be a concern of every citizen, and especially of those responsible for the safety and the disbursement of large amounts of money. The novice police officer can regard this book as a primer on fraud. The banker, the private attorney and the insurance executive should also be alerted to the possibilities of fraud if they are to function effectively.

The con artist may be a professional — a full-time dealer in stolen credit cards or a skilled forger. Or he may be a trusted employee, an embezzler hoping to cover his losses before they can be discovered. He may be a welsher who boosts his profits by the simple expedient of not paying his bills.

The only real defense against the con man is knowledge and a recognition of the fact that almost anyone can be fooled by a bunco artist — unless the intended victim knows a bit about the ploys and remembers to keep his guard up.

This book is as comprehensive and timeless as the authors have been able to make it. Doubtless, by the time it goes to press, hundreds of variations on the schemes described here will have been worked out by the nimble confidence men and women. However, it is hoped that once he knows the basic approaches used by the cons, the average citizen will be able to spot a bunk, and will know how to scream for help.

ACKNOWLEDGMENTS

ALL of the bunco schemes described in this book are based on reports in the files of local and federal law enforcement agencies. In every instance, the name or names of the victims and of the con artists have been changed.

The authors are especially grateful to the following individuals who have sent us case histories, given their time for interviews, and even read first drafts and offered special suggestions:

William Cushman, recently retired from the Los Angeles County Sheriff's Department; David P. Curnow, Assistant United States Attorney, San Diego, California; Chief Bernard L. Garmire and Lt. Herbert E. Netsch of the City of Miami Police Department, Miami, Florida; Deputy Morton L. Bardfield of the Suffolk County Sheriff's Department, Boston, Massachusetts; Bill Lendin of the Ventura County District Attorney's Office, Ventura, California; Carl Lane, recently retired from the Burbank, California, Police Force; Bill Hunter; Chuck Novac of United Air Lines; Major Wayne D. Ruch of the Columbus, Ohio, Division of Police; R. M. Sherman; Deputy District Attorney Barry M. Sax, Los Angeles.

CONTENTS

xi

A Compendium of Bunk
or
How To Spot a Con Artist

Chapter 1

CON GAMES —
THE WINNERS AND THE LOSERS

Bunco squad is another name for the forgery and frauds division of any law enforcement agency. All forgeries are by their very nature frauds, but not all frauds are forgeries. Frauds — also known as bunco games or bunks, confidence games or con games — come in an astounding and ever-increasing variety, and the bunco investigator needs to be as nimble of wit, and as alert to current trends, as the quick-moving confidence man.

The confidence man, so-called because of an almost uncanny ability to make his victims believe in him, also can sense opportunities in almost any situation. The energy crisis which struck the United States in 1973 was a terrible blow to the average citizen and the law-abiding businessman. To the bunco artist, it was a delightful new chance to make a quick buck. In no time, the unscrupulous cons were touting the virtues of makeshift gadgets to increase the gas mileage of the family car or stretch the heating capacity of the oil burner in the basement.

A newspaper report even hinting that minerals in drinking water might be hazardous to health will bring out the bunco artists in droves. If the current scare is the local water supply, they will be selling water softeners or water "purifiers."

At the moment when the most-desired object for the average American was a color television set, the fast-talking door-to-door operator specialized in color TV, either purchased through a supposedly legitimate channel or "stolen" and available to customers at a price they could not refuse.

So the detective whose work it is to locate and prosecute swindlers should do his homework: read the papers, keep up on the newest scares, fads and the latest version of the American dream.

There are several other things the bunco cop must do.

First, Forget Several Old Saws About Cheating an Honest

3

MAN. It's possible to hear even experienced police say, "You can't cheat a man who doesn't have a bit of larceny in his heart." This simply isn't true. The authors have found that the victims of bunco, the losers, can be as pure of heart as Abraham Lincoln. Certainly it is possible for the con man to take advantage of all the human frailties. He can exploit his victim's desire to get something for nothing or for very little. The lonely businessman who wants a little sex on the side (he is, after all, in Dubuque, and his wife is home in Altoona) can be made to pay dearly for his indiscretion. But so can the householder who wants nothing more than to protect his family from ill health or to get his roof fixed. The con artist's victim can be a sailor off a foreign ship who is induced to match coins with a stranger in a bar; or he can be a lonely, aging pensioner, frightened and bewildered, senile, sometimes physically intimidated. The retired schoolteacher with a small savings account can be reached through her greed, perhaps; but she can also be reached through her patriotism, her desire to help thwart a criminal, or simply through her kindliness.

The victims need not be simple-minded or financially unsophisticated. Doctors, lawyers, bankers, brokers and connoiseurs of fine art are taken in by the crooks every day. Businessmen who conduct their affairs with the greatest care in the world can be swindled systematically, and the amounts involved are often not small. The ambitious youngster who wants a career in selling, or in modeling or recording or television or the movies, is a prime target. So is the faded spinster who only wants to have her composition published by a music company, or the backyard tinkerer who has built a better mouse trap. The rich and the desperately poor, the sick and the healthy, old and young, all can be taken by a fast-buck operator.

The man on the bunco squad will, therefore, keep an open mind.

THE BUNCO DETECTIVE WILL ALSO LISTEN AND TAKE REPORTS. Except in special cases, it is difficult or impossible to bring criminal action against a slovenly or unscrupulous businessman unless it can be proved that he *intended* to defraud his customer. If the customer has unwisely paid too much for too little, he may simply have been guilty of poor judgment, and he may have no recourse except to sue. However, his complaint to the bunco squad will probably be his first contact with a law enforcement agency; and if his complaint is sloughed off too quickly, he will also surely become disillusioned with the police. He will leap to the conclusion that they don't care, really, what happens to the average John Doe. The bunco detective will have made an enemy, and he may need a friend. He should at least make out a report, carefully, in detail, of what has occurred. If he then receives additional similar complaints, he may see a pattern that indicates that all-important element, *intent*.

Sergeant William Cushman, of the Los Angeles County Sheriff's Department, cites the case of the silverware salesman as an example. This salesman, handling a perfectly respectable line of silverware which is sold door-to-door rather than through retail outlets, convinced a purchaser that he needed to borrow the set of flatware he had just sold him. An identical set was on order for a young couple who were to be married the next weekend, but it wouldn't arrive in time for the wedding. The newlyweds wanted to display the silver along with their other gifts at the reception.

The kindly and too-understanding purchasers of the silverware agreed to lend their forks and spoons and knives for the reception. The salesman departed with the silver, and when it should have been returned to the purchasers, it had been mysteriously lost.

The purchasers promptly contacted the bunco squad. They could have been told to sue the salesman. On the face of it, there was no intent to deprive them of their property. Anyone can have an accident. Anyone can lose silverware. The salesman might be legally responsible, but he didn't appear to be a criminal.

Not at first.

But the officer who interviewed the outraged pair who had lost their silverware took a report. A short time later there was another report from another couple who had purchased silver from the same man. Then another, and another and another. In every case, the salesman "borrowed" the newly-purchased silverware for display at a wedding reception.

There had been no wedding reception. It took very little investigation to discover that the silverware salesman had taken the "borrowed" silver to a pawn shop and then gone directly to the race track, where he immediately lost the money on the horses.

The fact that he was a bad handicapper was no defense. Because the reports were taken and the repetition of the pattern came through loud and clear, the man *intended* to swindle his customers. He *intended* to deprive them of property which was rightfully theirs; and he made misrepresentations, false statements, to accomplish this.

Ordinarily, for a conviction, there must be at least two witnesses to such statements or they must be in writing. However, when the pattern is repeated, when identical reports are made by persons who do not even know one another, there is no need for additional witnesses. The salesman intended to deprive his customers of property which was rightfully theirs, and he made false statements in order to do so. He was brought to trial on ten counts of fraud.

So the bunco investigators will keep up on the news, be alert, take reports and listen.

ALSO, HE WILL BE PATIENT. While doing research for this book, the author sat in one police department for twenty minutes and listened to a bunco cop talking to a woman who had called in to inquire about the legality of a chain letter.

If she fulfilled all the requirements set down in the letter, she reported, she hoped to collect $64,000 within two weeks. However, she most certainly did not want to run afoul of the postal inspectors.

The man on the bunco squad quietly advised her that chain letters soliciting money were illegal. He also read her, chapter and verse, the local statutes against any pyramid scheme instituted to gain money. Any person who set such a scheme in motion was guilty of a misdemeanor, he said.

The lady didn't want to break the law, but she wasn't averse to bending it slightly if there was a chance of getting $64,000 for practically nothing. The policeman advised her that he would not, in fact, get $64,000.

"Why not?" she demanded.

The policeman explained. She could not win because a chain letter operates on a pyramid principle and a pyramid expands too rapidly; she would soon run out of people. He went, almost step-by-step, through the mathematical progression of the chain.

"Well, maybe I could, if the chain isn't broken," she decided, ever hopeful.

He did not point out to her again that it was illegal; she was not that impressed by the mention of a misdemeanor. One must admit that "misdemeanor" doesn't sound nearly as daring as "felony." Or as wicked.

"You won't win," he assured her. "Only the people at the top of the pyramid, the people who start the letter going, can win. Everybody else loses."

"Don't you ever gamble?" she demanded.

"No," said the cop. "Gambling isn't legal here."

"Don't you ever go to Las Vegas and play the slot machines?" she asked.

"Yes. Sometimes I do. But gambling *is* legal in Nevada. Only I don't win and I know I'm not going to win, so I figure I'm just spending a little money for recreation and I let it go at that."

"But maybe you could win, and maybe..."

"On the chain letter, ma'am, you surely won't win, and it's a misdemeanor, like I said."

The policeman's voice had not gone up even a bit. He had remained composed throughout the conversation, which ended at last. The woman barely thanked him and she hung up on him.

And he put the telephone down, shrugged and said, "She doesn't believe me."

He refused to be saddened, because very often they don't believe him. "You can't let it spoil your day," he said briskly, and dismissed the incident and went on with his work.

So the bunco cop had been courteous, polite and patient; and a determined loser had refused to believe that she would be a loser, which meant that somewhere a bunch of con artists who had started that pyramid letter going had probably already collected bundles of dollar bills from people whose names they picked out of a telephone directory. Does this make the con men the winners?

In the case of the chain letter, they may have won that time. By the time the lady who had such fierce trust in her chances of getting something for nothing called the bunco squad, the names of the men who set the letter up in the first place would almost surely have been lost.

Many times the bunco artist does win because no one calls the police, but very few win forever. Bunco detectives who have worked for many years apprehending those who steal by fraud admit to a certain respect for the con man. They are clever. They are often charming. They do have that ability to convince their victims. The schemes they work out can be ingenious. However, according to most policemen, if they put the same amount of work and care into any legitimate enterprise, they'd be rich and free. Instead of that, they eventually wind up broke and in jail.

One first-class pigeon drop artist, a woman who has operated her bunco game in cities from one coast to the other, can make more than $10,000 a day performing her specialty. Does she have a closet filled with mink coats and a safe deposit box filled with diamonds? No, she doesn't. She has a man about whom she is completely nuts, and he gets the money. She may clear $12,000 on Tuesday and on Wednesday she may, in desperation, turn prostitute for twenty dollars a trick.

Not only doesn't she have a closet filled with mink coats; she doesn't even have a closet. She can't settle anywhere since she's always wanted and she's always on the run. She does time now and then. The police know her. Everywhere, they know her. So she's a loser, too.

They all are. They could go legitimate and make it, but they really can't.

What is the secret of the con man? Why does he do it the crooked way, when straight is only sensible? Because he has a twist. He has to think he can fool the ordinary, run-of-the-mill John Doe. He has to think he's smarter.

So con games are games where no one wins. Everyone who plays is a loser.

Chapter 2

THE PIGEON DROP —
THE ALL-TIME FAVORITE

ALL dictionaries give several definitions for the word "pigeon." A pigeon is a bird. A pigeon is also a term of endearment. It is another word for a pretty girl. To the confidence man, the pigeon is a sucker, a dupe, an easy mark; and the pigeon drop is probably the most frequently practiced con in America. Possibly it is the most frequently practiced con anywhere.

Also, although it is a "short" con, a comparatively simple swindle, the pigeon drop is one of the most difficult to explain to the layman. The average person just won't believe that it will work.

It works.

Mrs. Annie Goldman was the classic pigeon drop victim. An ultra-respectable widow who had seen her seventieth birthday, she was looking forward to celebrating her seventy-first with her children and grandchildren. One morning in May — an unusually bright morning for foggy San Francisco — she was sitting on a bench on Lincoln Way waiting for a bus.

A woman approached Mrs. Goldman, sat down beside her on the bench, and sighed. It was a weary sigh, and Mrs. Goldman turned and regarded the woman with mild curiosity. The woman was a good twenty years Mrs. Goldman's junior, and some ten pounds heavier than she should have been. Her white uniform, white stockings, and the sensible, rubber-soled white shoes she wore indicated that she worked at the University of California Medical Center up the hill. Her tan coat was slightly worn, and the brown handbag she held on her lap was shabby.

She glanced at Mrs. Goldman and smiled, and her broad face took on a somewhat rueful look. "It's a shame to have to work on a day like this," she said.

Mrs. Goldman only nodded. Mrs. Goldman's older son, Ben, often expressed irritation with her because she readily talked to

9

strangers.

"If all the days were like this," said the woman, "I'd move here for good."

Mrs. Goldman felt she couldn't sit in churlish silence in the presence of this kindly-appearing individual. Besides, Ben didn't understand. She was often lonely in the small apartment she had rented after her husband's death. So few people had time for an elderly woman.

"You don't live here?" asked Mrs. Goldman.

"Not really," said the woman in white. "I've got an apartment in Los Angeles. Though I'd move up here and give San Francisco a try. I sublet my place for a couple of months. We'll see how it goes."

"You're a nurse?" said Mrs. Goldman.

"Not really. I mean, I'm not an R.N. I'm a practical nurse. But that's all right. There's always a place open for a practical nurse. I can move around if I feel like it. Never lack for work. And idle hands..."

Mrs. Goldman smiled. "Yes, I know."

The woman leaned forward and rubbed the calf of her leg as if it hurt. "I haven't really had time to get settled here yet," she said, "but I found a job right away, and a nice enough place to live for the time being. It's only ten minutes away on the bus. My friends didn't want me to come here. They said, 'Carrie' — that's my name, Carrie Fidler — they said, 'Carrie, why go up there? It's cold and damp in San Francisco and you don't know anyone.' But I'm not worried. I've started out alone in lots of places and I've always made friends easily. It's a good life." She grinned. "Okay, as long as my legs hold out," she said.

Mrs. Goldman nodded. Of course, a practical nurse would be fine, as long as her legs held out.

"You can't really count on that though, can you?" said Carrie Fidler. "I always keep a little something in reserve, you know."

"Yes," said Mrs. Goldman. "I can see... yes, we all have to do that, I suppose."

Mrs. Goldman was aware of a movement then, behind the bench, and someone said, "Did one of you ladies drop this?"

Mrs. Goldman turned. A pert and pretty young black woman

stood beside the bench. She wore a lime green coat with an imitation fur collar.

"Beg pardon?" said Carrie Fidler.

The young woman held out a bulky envelope. "This was under the bench," she said. "Is it yours?"

Carried Fidler took the envelope and glanced at it without any special show of interest. It was slightly bigger than an ordinary business envelope, and unmarked, except for a few smudges. "Not mine," said Carrie Fidler, and she handed it to Mrs. Goldman.

"Not mine, either," said Mrs. Goldman. She turned the envelope over. The flap was unsealed. Almost without thinking, Mrs. Goldman opened the envelope and looked inside.

"Good heavens!" she said.

"What is it?" asked Carrie Fidler.

Her hands trembling slightly, Mrs. Goldman bent toward Carrie Fidler. The black girl in the green coat leaned over the two older women and watched as Mrs. Goldman thumbed through the money in the envelope. Carried Fidler looked around. The street was almost empty. There were only herself, the girl in the green coat and Mrs. Goldman. Passing by, walking briskly, was a young girl in denims — a young girl who didn't even carry a handbag, and who couldn't possibly have dropped an envelope filled with money.

Carrie Fidler took the envelope from Mrs. Goldman and carefully counted the bills inside. "Six thousand dollars!" she exclaimed. She counted again. "Six thousand dollars in five-hundred dollar bills."

She took a piece of paper out of the envelope and read aloud: "Phil, please keep this until the IRS is off my back. Damned if they're going to get it. W."

The three women were silent for several seconds. Then the black girl spoke up. "IRS! That's the Internal Revenue Service. Someone's cheating on the income tax!" There was a jubilant note in her voice.

Carrie Fidler pursed her lips and her bland face was suddenly flushed with outrage. "It's probably sinful money. It's probably from something illegal, like the numbers of the races or something."

"Sinful or not, it's money," crowed the black girl. "I found it and I can use it."

Carried Fidler fixed the girl with a righteous stare. "You picked it up," she announced. "This lady here opened it and I . . . I counted it."

Mrs. Goldman cleared her throat. "The money really belongs to the man who wrote that note," she pointed out. "He was letting the person called Phil hold it for him."

"Finders, keepers!" snapped the black girl.

"We should take the money to the police station," said Mrs. Goldman. "We should turn it in to lost and found."

"We take that to the police, we never see it again!" cried the black girl. "And that Phil, if he's hiding it from the tax people, he's not going to no police station to get it."

Again the three were silent. Carried Fidler still held the envelope.

"Look," said the black girl at last, "I know a lawyer I can call. He's an old friend and he'll tell me right. We don't want no fuss. Let me call him and let him decide, huh?"

Carrie Fidler still sat firm and still held the envelope.

"If you're so worried, you can come with me and you can hold the money while I call my friend. Okay, lady?"

Carrie looked at Mrs. Goldman. "I guess that makes sense," she said. "Why don't we do that? We can go with . . . with this girl and wait while she calls her friend. There's a coffee shop over there. What do you say?"

Mrs. Goldman slowly nodded. The woman named Carrie Fidler hadn't actually said so, but her meaning was clear. She meant that all three might actually have a claim to that money. Mrs. Goldman had never in her life committed an illegal act. She didn't intend to do so now. Still, if the black girl's lawyer said it was all right. . .

Dazzled, she thought of what she might do with part of that money. Little Simon, her grandson, needed braces on his teeth. She could pay for them and still have enough left for a down payment on a car for her son, Ben. Ben really needed a new car.

Mrs. Goldman followed Carrie Fidler and the black girl, who introduced herself as Melba Branwell, to the coffee shop near the bus stop. Mrs. Fidler took a table near the door and Mrs. Goldman sat across from her, and they both sipped at too-hot, bitter coffee while Melba Branwell went to the telephone booth and shut herself in. They heard the coin Melba slipped into the telephone slot clang home and they saw Melba dial. She talked at some length, then pushed a second dime into the slot and talked some more. At last she hung up.

"My lawyer friend says not to worry," Melba told them when she came back to the table. "He says since the envelope wasn't mailed, with a stamp and all, it isn't like we were taking from the post office. We don't know who Phil is, or who asked him to hold the money. We could turn it over to the cops, but the lawyer said, like I do, that Phil or that other guy won't go to the cops and ask for money they're hiding from the tax people. My friend says we can keep it. He said share it three ways."

"Six thousand dollars," said Mrs. Goldman.

"That's two thousand for each of us," said Carrie.

Mrs. Goldman decided that after she'd paid for Simon's dental work and put a down payment on a new car for Ben, there'd be enough left for a new stole to wear to the Thursday night bingo games.

"I know what I'm going to do with my share," said Carrie. "I'm going to give it to the church. Love of money is the root of all evil."

Mrs. Goldman smiled. The money wouldn't be an evil to her. She wouldn't have it long enough for it to be evil.

Carrie Fidler's eyes flicked over Melba Branwell and her pretty cocoa-colored face and her green coat with its imitation fur collar. She seemed to dismiss Melba as one lost beyond recall. Obviously Melba would take her part of the money and do something unsavory, or at least frivolous. But Carrie touched Mrs. Goldman's hand. "Mrs. Goldman, why don't you let me give your share to the church, too? Believe me, you don't want that money. It'll bring you nothing but trouble."

"Oh, sure!" said Melba.

Carrie ignored her. "It's for your own good, Mrs. Goldman," she said. "I like you and I wouldn't want to see you get into trouble. If you're not used to that kind of money, it can be a weight around your neck. It can drag you down!"

"Look who's talkin'!" snapped Melba. "You're pretty high and mighty, Mrs. Carrie Fidler, worried about Mrs. Goldman for fear she can't take care of herself. You don't look to me like you have any money. You don't look like you *ever* had any money. You hate the stuff so much, why should we share with you? Maybe you'll be the one to get into trouble."

"I have money." Carrie's voice was low, almost hoarse.

"Like two thousand dollars? demanded Melba.

"Certainly. I work steady. I always work and I put something by for a rainy day."

"You better make up your mind it's raining today," said Melba. "You better show me. And you, too, Mrs. Goldman. If we're all going to worry about each other's souls, show me how terrific you are at handling money. After all..." Melba's voice dripped with sarcasm, "... after all, you're such a nice lady. I wouldn't want you to get hurt."

"Oh, I *am* used to money," said Mrs. Goldman quickly. "Before my husband died, I handled all our money. The last car we bought cost over four thousand dollars."

"Where's the car?" said Melba.

Mrs. Goldman drooped. "I had to get rid of it," she admitted. "I never did drive. Besides, it needed work and it seemed smarter to have a little emergency fund and..."

"And you're broke," said Melba.

"No! No, I'm not. I have some income and savings and..."

"Show me," demanded Melba.

"My bankbook's at home," said Mrs. Goldman. "I can get it and..."

"No bankbook," decided Melba. "Anybody can flash a bankbook. You could even borrow one. Cash. I want to see cash. Two thousand dollars. Otherwise you can deal yourself out. I *did* spot the envelope, you know."

The black girl then glared at Carrie Fidler. "And you," she said. "Two thousand? I don't believe you ever say two thousand in one piece in your life!"

"I have it!" said Carrie firmly. "I moved part of my account here. You'll see. I'll get my checkbook."

"Okay, you get it and you write your check for two thousand and you bring the money. We'll meet here in an hour, okay?"

Carrie stiffened. "How do I know you'll show up?"

"You don't, do you?" said Melba. "Only I'll stick with Mrs. Goldman and I'll have the six thousand with me, so I know *you'll* show."

Carrie hesitated for a second, then got out of the booth. "An hour?" she said.

"On the button," said Melba.

Carrie Fidler left the coffee shop.

"She's too much!" declared Melba. "Money's the root of all evil, but she wants it so bad she can taste it. Come on, Mrs. Goldman. Stick with me and we can go to your bank. We'll show your money to that...that holier-than-thou and get it back into the bank before closing time."

Suddenly warmed by Melba's show of friendliness, Mrs. Goldman let the girl accompany her to her apartment and then to her bank, where Melba waited outside while Mrs. Goldman withdrew two thousand dollars from her savings account. The bills were new and crisp, and Mrs. Goldman put them into her purse, in the side pocket which closed with a zipper. Half an hour later, Melba and Mrs. Goldman were back in the coffee shop, sipping more black coffee and waiting — and waiting and waiting. And the woman named Carrie Fidler did not appear.

The appointed hour passed and Melba became restless.

"Maybe she didn't understand," she said. She and Mrs. Goldman were both sitting so that they could face the street. Mrs. Goldman saw a bus sail by and she heard it stop at the corner.

"She could be on that bus," said Melba.

But still Carrie Fidler didn't appear.

"Or she could be waiting outside," Melba decided.

Mrs. Goldman nodded. "I'll go and see," she offered, and she got up and started toward the door.

"Your purse!" Melba picked Mrs. Goldman's purse off the floor, where Mrs. Goldman had put it, and held it out to her and her voice dropped. "You have two thousand in it, remember?" she warned. "Don't leave it here. I've got to go to the ladies room."

"Oh!" Mrs. Goldman took the purse from Melba and tucked it

under her arm. She went to the door of the coffee shop, looked out, then went out onto the street.

There was no sight of the woman called Carrie.

Mrs. Goldman went back into the coffee shop, sat down and waited for Melba to come back from the ladies room.

Melba never came back. After a time, Mrs. Goldman, uneasy, opened her purse. The zipper on that special little side compartment was open. The compartment was empty. The two thousand dollars was gone.

Carrie Fidler was gone.

The girl named Melba was gone, out through the door marked "Exit" which was right next to the restrooms.

Mrs. Annie Goldman, widow, mother, grandmother, upright citizen, had been the typical victim of a typical pair of pigeon drop artists.

WHY IS MRS. GOLDMAN'S A TYPICAL CASE? WHY IS AN ELDERLY WOMAN IN SOMEWHAT REDUCED CIRCUMSTANCES USUALLY THE VICTIM? Elderly women in somewhat reduced circumstances are the ones who do have money — real money — in the bank. They are not paying off debts incurred for new furniture or new cars. They usually have some small inheritance from a deceased spouse. They are fearful of illness and they are fearful of being a burden on their children. They want a little something put by, and they will scrimp and save to get it. They need the security.

And, after years of scrimping and saving and planning and budgeting, they can be intoxicated at the thought of a sudden windfall. If they possess even the tiniest iota of greed, it can be excited so that they forget, for the moment, the habits of a lifetime.

WHO ARE THE TYPICAL PIGEON DROP ARTISTS? The woman called Carrie Fidler and the young black girl called Melba are prototypes. Dozens of teams like them are operating around the country. Usually a pigeon drop team consists of a Caucasian and a member of some other ethnic group. The victim is thus more easily convinced that the two con artists do not know each other.

One of the women makes the initial approach. In this case, it was Carrie Fidler, the Caucasian — not too young and appearing most respectable. She engages the victim in conversation.

The second bunco artist "finds" the money in the envelope.

The money is almost always accompanied by a note such as the one indicating that the man named Phil was hiding funds from the Internal Revenue Service. Sometimes the money is accompanied by betting slips, or some other papers that indicate that it is the proceeds of prostitution. This lulls the victim into forgetting, for the moment, that finders are not legally keepers. The victim believes that the money has been gained by illicit means — gotten by evil men. There does not seem to be much point in restoring ill-gotten gains to such creatures. A trio of virtuous women would do much more good with that money.

Sometimes one of the con artists pretends to telephone a lawyer. Often there is no such pretense. Sometimes there isn't any questioning of the victim's ability to handle cash safely, as in the case of Mrs. Goldman. So dazzling is the skill of the practiced pigeon drop operators that a victim can be induced to part with her life savings only to show "good faith," whatever that may mean. So confident does the victim become in the swindlers that she may not have to have her pocket picked, as Mrs. Goldman did. She may hand over her cash to one of the bunco artists so that it can be shown to a third party. If she does not have $2,000, as Mrs. Goldman did, the con artists will settle for whatever she does have. A few hundred is better than nothing, and this particular game is a "light bunk" — a quick one, requiring little preparation once the basic routine is worked out. Less than two hours passed between the time Mrs. Goldman was engaged in conversation on that bus bench by the woman named Carrie and the time Mrs. Goldman realized that she had lost $2,000 of her precious savings. Carrie and Melba would gladly have squandered two hours for a couple of hundred, if that was all Mrs. Goldman had.

THERE ARE ENDLESS VARIATIONS ON THE THEME. In one suburban supermarket, a seventy-four-year-old woman was approached by a fiftyish matron. They both commented on the high cost of living. Then the younger woman introduced a friend who was in a high state of excitement. The friend claimed that she had found $8,000 in an envelope in the parking lot of the shopping center. The envelope containing the money also contained a note indicating that the $8,000 was a payoff being made by a bookmaker. The woman who had "found" the money convinced the aged victim that she worked for a loan company, and that she had been advised by her supervisor that she could keep the money and share it with her friends. The victim quickly became a "friend," withdrew almost $1,500 from two different bank accounts, turned it over to the two bunco artists, and waited patiently in the parking lot of the shopping center so that the two con women could show the "good faith" money to the supervisor at the loan company.

Only after an hour did the victim become suspicious and drive to the loan company. She asked to see the supervisor. He did not and had never known the con artists and he knew nothing of any "found" money. He called the police.

In a reputable department store in one of the wealthier suburbs of Boston, a grandmother was approached and asked for advice about the selection of a gift for a new baby girl. She was happy to give her advice. She was even happier when a third party wandered along with an envelope full of "found" money. Although the kindly grandmother was not in need, she went to her bank and withdrew $3000 from her savings account to show her good faith. The con women switched the bank envelope containing her cash for one containing cut-up pages from an old copy of *Reader's Digest*.

Elderly women are the typical victims, but they are not the only victims. In star-studded Beverly Hills, a young woman was approached by a well-dressed matron who admired the pin the young woman was wearing. While the two chatted, they were approached by a third woman who had "found" an envelope containing cash and some betting slips.

In this case, the young matron had her guard up. She left the scene immediately and she called the police. The con women were not apprehended. They moved too fast even for the Beverly Hills Police Department.

Sometimes men are the pigeons. In one large Florida city, a thirty-eight-year-old male bartender was standing on a corner trying to hail a cab when two men approached him and started a conversation. They told him they wanted to get a girl. The bartender was sympathetic to the point of participation. He decided he wanted a girl, too. The men convinced him that since they were going into a tough area, they should put all their money together and one would hold it for the others. Each of the three men produced cash, and one suspect wrapped it in a piece of newspaper. The victim was induced to hold the money for the other two while they visited a house of prostitution. After they came back, it would be the victim's turn to get a girl. The bunco artists never returned, and when the victim opened the newspaper there was no money. The packages had been switched while his attention was distracted. The bartender lost $720 on that swindle. He had planned to purchase a movie projector, and the cash he had in his pockets was almost every cent he possessed.

According to Miami police, this is the way the bunco game called the pigeon drop originated; the victim was induced to believe that he would have sex.

There are hundreds, perhaps thousands, of variations on the pigeon drop. There is one constant factor, and that is greed. The victims were willing to gamble for an unearned buck (or, in the case of the victimized bartender, for a fling with a prostitute). The con artists were able to exploit this failing and get the victims to withdraw money, or hand it over, to prove that the victim knew how to handle money or to show "good faith" or to safeguard funds by pooling them.

The pigeon drop is extremely difficult to explain to the layman because most laymen who have not encountered con men cannot believe that a sane individual will take money out of the bank at the urging of a perfect stranger. The fact is that people who are otherwise sane, but have that grain of avarice, do it every day.

THE BEST DEFENSE AGAINST THE PIGEON DROP ARTIST IS EDUCATION. In Los Angeles, the police department sponsors neighborhood meetings at which detectives from various divisions lecture on how the citizen can protect himself from the criminal. Bunco schemes have been discussed at these meetings, and films on bunco have been shown. These films are most effective, since the average John Doe has to actually see a dramatization of a pigeon drop to believe it.

In some cities, the law enforcement agencies have gotten the cooperation of the banks. Tellers cannot refuse to release funds to a depositor who has money in a savings account. However, instead of releasing large amounts of cash, some savings institutions put a limit on the amount of cash a depositor withdraws and make up the balance by issuing a certified check. In this way, the bite the bunco artist takes is not as large. He or she will not usually be interested in a check.

News media can help, although probably not much. If a pigeon drop team is operating in an area, the local citizens should be warned not to withdraw funds from a bank for display to strangers and not to discuss their finances with strangers.

Above all, the victims should not be embarrassed. Take the reports without displaying scorn and pray for victims with a good eye for detail and a retentive memory. The case of Mrs. Annie Goldman is typical (and Goldman is *not* the victim's real name) and in that case the police were lucky. Mrs. Goldman did have an eye for detail, and the cashier in the coffee shop where the three women had waited and talked could also provide descriptions of "Carrie Fidler" and "Melba Branwell." The descriptions went out over the wire. The next day, a plainclothesman in Oakland saw a woman answering Carrie's description chatting with an elderly lady near Merritt Hospital. The woman was dressed as a nurse. When a young Negro girl moved in and attempted to hand the woman in white an envelope, the detective moved in, too — near enough to trail the intended victim to her bank. The woman who had called herself Carrie and the girl with the pretty, cocoa-brown face and the pert manner were pulled into the Oakland police station.

The print-out on "Carrie" covered three single-spaced pages. She had begun her career in Cleveland, where she was a prostitute. She had perfected her pigeon drop routine in New York, with the help of an older accomplice. She had been working at prostitution or pigeon drop or both ever since the forties. She had recruited Melba in a bar in Baltimore and had trained her, and the pair had been working together for three months.

The print-out on "Melba" wasn't long. She had been arrested a few times for soliciting. But then, Melba was still young. She would be around again.

Chapter 3

THE BANK EXAMINER IS CALLING

LITTLE kids used to play cops and robbers. They took turns being the good guys who caught the bad guys. Today, they are more apt to watch the good guys and the bad guys fight it out on television. But still, even among grown people, the thrill of helping nab an evil-doer can be an occasional daydream. If the telephone rings in the home of a law-abiding citizen, and that citizen is asked by a bank official, or by an agency as prestigious as the FBI, to become a sort of secret agent to trap an embezzling bank teller, the citizen may be eager, willing and delighted to do his or her part.

This admirable quirk of human nature makes the bank examiner swindle a very lucrative con game.

Miss Evalina Johnson was a law-abiding citizen. A retired schoolteacher, she lived modestly on her pension. She refused to be tempted by worldly goods which were beyond her means; she banked a part of her income each month in case some emergency might arise.

One morning, as she finished her second cup of coffee, Miss Johnson's telephone rang.

"Miss Evalina Johnson?" said a brisk female voice.

"Yes," said Miss Johnson.

"You are Miss Evalina Johnson who lives at 1481 Elmwood Road?" asked the woman on the telephone. The voice sounded young.

Miss Johnson confirmed it.

"This is Miss Parkinson at the Atwater Pacific Bank," said the young woman on the telephone. "Miss Johnson, there seems to be some question about your account and..."

Miss Johnson seldom interrupted other people, but in this case she made an exception. "There certainly must be some question," she said firmly. "I don't have an account at Atwater Pacific. I bank with Security First."

"Oh?" The young lady was no longer so brisk. "But it wasn't your checking account, Miss Johnson. Your savings account..."

"My savings account is with Security First," Miss Johnson informed her caller.

"That would be — let's see — the branch at Elmwood and Third?" questioned Miss Parkinson.

"That's correct."

"Well, there surely is a mix-up, Miss Johnson. I'll have our vice president call Mr. Cooper at Security First. I'm sure Mr. Cooper will be getting in touch with you shortly. Thank you very much, Miss Johnson."

Miss Johnson felt extremely uneasy when she put down the telephone. What had she to do with the Atwater Pacific Bank, and why was the brisk Miss Parkinson going to call Mr. Cooper at her own bank?

Before many minutes passed, the telephone rang again. A deep male voice introduced itself as belonging to Mr. Cooper of Security First National Bank. "We've had a telephone call from a vice president at Atwater Pacific, Miss Johnson," said Mr. Cooper. "This is a very embarrassing admission to have to make, but it appears that one of our tellers is manipulating some of our less active savings account. I wonder if I could trouble you to get your passbook. I'd like to check the balance shown there with what we have on our records."

Miss Johnson's hands were suddenly wet. She went to the bureau where she kept her passbook. She found it in its usual place in the top drawer and hurried back to the telephone.

"Mr. Cooper?" she said.

"Yes. Now that's account number...?"

"Number 14325," said Miss Johnson obligingly.

"Number 14325. Yes, that's correct. And the balance shown in your passbook?"

"Four thousand, six hundred dollars," said Miss Johnson, "and eighty-three cents."

"Ah, yes. That would include the interest computed for the last quarter. Very good, Miss Johnson. Now, there's not a thing for you to worry about. Remember, your funds are insured by the federal government. Your money is perfectly safe."

Miss Johnson was happy to hear this.

"It's a great deal to ask, Miss Johnson," Mr. Cooper went on. "However, we will need the cooperation of at least one of our depositors. We're reasonably sure we know who the embezzler is, but we need proof. Would you be free to come down to the bank today?"

Miss Johnson would be free. "Shall I ask for you, Mr. Cooper?" she said.

"Under no circumstances," said Mr. Cooper firmly. "That would arouse suspicion immediately. No. If you can, arrive at about 10:45. The teller will be back from coffee by that time. Go to the fourth window from the left and withdraw — let's see, your balance is over four thousand — withdraw three thousand. Ask for the money in fifties and twenties. That will amount to quite a bulky package, so be sure to bring a large handbag. When you have the money, take a taxi and go directly home. Don't worry about anything. We don't want anything to happen to you or to your money, and we've called in the FBI on this case. Your cab will be followed. After you get home, you'll be called upon by an agent of the Federal Bureau. He'll show you his identification. Make sure you see that identification before you turn the money over to him."

"Turn the money over to him?" echoed Miss Johnson.

"He'll keep it only long enough to list the serial numbers and to treat it with a special chemical," explained Mr. Cooper. "It's a chemical that is invisible in ordinary light, but it turns blue under ultraviolent light, you see."

Miss Johnson didn't understand, really, but it sounded thrillingly like something out of a mystery on the late-late show.

"After the serial numbers have been recorded and the money has been treated, it will be returned to you. Call a cab and come immediately to the bank to redeposit the money. Will you do that, Miss Johnson? Of course, we'll be happy to reimburse you for your expenses, and naturally there will be no penalty for withdrawing the money so far as interest goes."

"I'll get dressed right away," said Miss Johnson.

At exactly 10:45, Miss Johnson was in the bank presenting her passbook and a withdrawal slip for three thousand dollars to the young woman who presided over the fourth window from the left at Security First. She asked for the money in fifties and twenties. The girl excused herself and went to consult one of her superiors about this unusually large withdrawal.

The young teller soon returned and counted wads of bills for Miss Johnson. She then had Miss Johnson count the money. Assured that she had given Miss Johnson the correct amount, the young woman made the appropriate notes in the passbook and stamped the withdrawal slip. She smiled, warned Miss Johnson about being careful with all that cash, and watched Miss Johnson leave the bank, clutching her handbag close under her arm.

There was a taxi at the stand right outside of the bank. Miss Johnson took it, and noticed with satisfaction that a dark green sedan pulled away from the curb just behind the cab. The sedan trailed the taxi to Miss Johnson's apartment house, then passed the cab and parked half a block down the street.

Miss Johnson paid the cabby and hurried to her apartment. She had not taken her hat off before there was a knock on the door. When she opened the door, cautiously, with the chain still on, she confronted a tidy young man in a business suit. He was clean-cut, scrubbed and wholesome. He gave her an immaculate, hearty smile and produced the proper identification. Miss Johnson had to assume that it was the proper identification. His card did have the seal of the federal government. She glimpsed a scrawled signature and a photograph of the young man. It all looked very official.

The young man took the money from Miss Johnson, wrote a receipt for it, thanked her warmly for her cooperation in preventing a serious embezzlement, and promised to return the money to her by two at the latest, so that she would have ample time to redeposit it in the bank before closing time.

The young agent then departed. He did not return.

By 2:15, Miss Johnson was extremely worried about her money. She called her bank and asked to speak to Mr. Cooper. No one at the Elmwood branch of the bank had ever heard of Mr. Cooper.

Miss Johnson then called the police.

MISS JOHNSON HAD BEEN THE VICTIM OF THE BANK EXAMINER SWINDLE, AND SHE REPRESENTS THE TYPICAL VICTIM OF THIS BUNK.

Like Mrs. Goldman, who fell for the pigeon drop scheme, she was an elderly woman, living alone, and she had money put by in case of an emergency. Unlike Mrs. Goldman, she was not motivated by greed. She wanted only to do her bit, to help fight crime.

THE MO OF CONFIDENCE MEN USING THE BANK EXAMINER SWINDLE VARIES ALMOST NOT AT ALL. These con artists select their victims after they have pinpoined the location of banks and savings institutions in any city on a map. They then go through the telephone directory and underline listings which are in women's names. Since telephone directories include street addresses, they can make fairly accurate guesses as to the banks where these women might have accounts.

In Miss Johnson's case, the woman who called herself Miss Parkinson made the initial call. If she mentioned the right bank on the first try, she advised the victims that "Our Mr. Cooper will be calling you shortly." If the bank she mentioned on that first call was not the bank in which the intended victim kept her funds, she usually had no difficulty in getting the name of the right bank from the victim.

If a man answered the telephone, or if the victim indicated that she would have to consult with a husband, son or nephew, the woman usually terminated the conversation, explaining that it was a "misunderstanding." Although men have been taken in by this scheme, the con artists prefer to avoid dealing with a man.

The second telephone call, the call made by "Mr. Cooper," was to ascertain how big the haul could be and to persuade the victim to help the forces of law and order.

Says one police detective, "The standard process for con men working the bank examiner dodge is to phone the victim back immediately after giving the instructions on how to pick up the money. If the phone is busy, the caper is off. The con man figures the victim is calling the police to set something up, and he goes on to another victim. Even if the woman is calling a bridge friend to tell her the exciting news and the line is busy, she'll never hear from Mr. Cooper again, and also she'll never see the bag man."

The bag man is usually the only member of the confidence ring that the victim does see. He is the wholesome young man with the forged credentials who actually collects the money from the victim.

In Miss Johnson's case, the bunco squad had very little to go on. The bag man, that immaculate impersonator of an FBI agent, was so average that he might have been manufactured out of plastic. Miss Johnson had a retentive memory, and she had automatically noted the number on the license plate of the green sedan which had trailed the taxi to her apartment. It was a habit she had acquired after watching many detective shows on television. The police checked out the license number. The car belonged to an auto rental agency and had been taken out that morning by a young man whose description matched that given by Miss Johnson. The young man had all the proper identification, but the driver's license which he showed the clerk must have been forged. The Bureau of Motor Vehicles had no record of such a license. The credit card which he had presented was a stolen card, and the car was found two days later, abandoned on a dead-end street and wiped clean of fingerprints.

In the meantime, four more reports came into the bunco division from helpful ladies who had withdrawn their money from the bank to help trap a suspected embezzler. Warnings went out to the press and to the banks and then, on the third day, the bunco squad got a break.

A widow who had a savings account in the First Street branch of the Western Savings and Loan had had the usual conversation with "Mr. Cooper," an officer of that institution. After unwittingly confiding her account number and balance to him, she actually left her home to make her withdrawal, and then had second thoughts about the entire affair. She did not read the newspapers, but she did recall that never before had the bank called her to verify her balance; she had always called the bank. She did call the bank from a pay station and asked to speak to Mr. Cooper. When she learned of the nonexistence of that person, she promptly called the police.

The quick-witted widow made her withdrawal, as Mr. Cooper had suggested. She took a cab back to her home on West Elvira Street, also as Mr. Cooper had suggested, and this time the cab was followed by a light gray sedan. When the personable young driver of the sedan presented his FBI credentials and collected the swag, he walked out of the widow's house and into the arms of two members of the bunco squad.

The bag man, hoping for a break in court, led the bunco men to a furnished apartment not far from Miss Johnson's own flat, and there the forces of law and order did catch up with "Mr. Cooper" and the brisk and efficient "Miss Parkinson." They had finished conducting their telephone survey on the financial resources of the neighborhood and were packing to leave. They had made one very serious blunder; they had remained in the area one day too long.

Chapter 4

THE GOOD SAMARITANS

THERE is a swindle which is identical to the classic pigeon drop described in Chapter 2 except for one very important factor: the victim is a good and generous individual without a smidgin of greed in his soul.

Father Juan Perez discovered this on the Monday following the annual fiesta at his church. Father Perez was tired that Monday morning, but happy. His building fund was richer by $10,173.25. There had been months of planning for the fiesta, then two days of frenzy, with dancing in the schoolyard and games and booths and a bake sale and a white elephant sale. There had been no sleep on Sunday night because Father Perez and the parish finance committee had had to count every penny they had taken in. Then, on Monday morning, the great event was over. The cash was in the bank and Father Perez could relax.

On that Monday morning, Father Perez was informed by his housekeeper that there was a man in the parlor who wanted to see him.

The man was a stranger to Father Perez. He was more than middle-aged, and dressed in a suit which was too warm and too formal for free-wheeling California in the spring. Also, he had a hat. Few of Father Perez' flock owned hats.

"I've come about my sister," said the man. "You may know her. She's Mrs. Goldstein."

Father Perez frowned. He could not think of a single Goldstein in his parish.

"She lives on First Street." The man spoke quickly, like a penitent in the confessional, eager to get the thing over. "She's in this parish or . . . or she would be if she hadn't married that Jew. She was taken sick last Friday and she's in the hospital. Heart attack. They may have to do open-heart surgery. She had them send for me and I flew in from Detroit last night. I'm sorry. I didn't introduce myself. My name's Henry Kelly and I'm her only living

28

relative."

"Her husband...?" began Father Perez.

"He's dead. He died last year. She married out of the church, you know, Father, and now she's facing this thing and she wants to come back. She wants to see a priest. She asked me if I could get you. She knows you, you see, even if you don't know her."

"How many years has it been?" asked Father Perez.

"More than twenty," said Kelly.

Father Perez was troubled. "It will be a complication. I think the chancery..."

"There may not be time," said Kelly quickly.

"She is dying?"

"I don't know. They won't say, or they can't say. I talked to the doctor last night and again this morning. She could come through the operation and live to be a hundred, or she could go out like that!" Kelly snapped his fingers.

"I see. Which hospital?"

Kelly named the place. It was not one of the largest hospitals in Los Angeles County, but it wasn't one of the smallest, either. It was less than three miles from St. Theresa's Church.

"I will meet you there," said Father Perez. "Or do you have a car?"

"I came in a cab," said Kelly.

"Then I will drive you," said the priest, and he went to get his stole and his crucifix and the holy oils for anointing.

At the hospital, the two men took the elevator to the third floor, where Kelly suggested that the priest remain in the waiting room while he went to see that his sister was awake. He was back in less than a minute.

"They took her downstairs for some tests," he reported. "It'll be an hour. Can I buy you a cup of coffee, Father?"

He could, and he and the priest went down to the first floor and found the coffee shop, which was almost deserted in mid-morning. They took a table near the door and ordered coffee. Father Perez sipped his; Kelly did no more than stir his about with a spoon.

"I wish she'd sent for me sooner," said Kelly.

Father Perez took refuge in his native tongue. He murmured in

Spanish of the will of God.

"Padre?" It was the man at the next table — a sickly looking person who was so thin that his clothes seemed scarcely to touch him. "Padre, you speak Spanish?"

Father Perez admitted that he did, that he was from Mexico.

Without apology, the thin man picked up his milk shake and joined Kelly and Father Perez at their table. He began to talk in a rapid patter of Spanish quite unlike the Spanish of Father Perez' homeland, but still comprehensible to the priest. He was, he said, Hector Romero, lately come to Los Angeles from Caracas, Venezuela. He had need of an agent — a bonded person, completely trustworthy — to handle for him a matter most delicate.

Senor Romero looked questioningly at Kelly.

"I do not believe Mr. Kelly speaks Spanish," said Father Perez.

"No, I don't," said Kelly. "What's this guy's problem?"

"He needs a commissionary — an agent," said the priest.

"It is very confidential," said Romero in Spanish. He went on then, and told of his mission. His father in Caracas was dying. He had sent for a priest to make his confession, and he had confessed a thing that had troubled him always. Romero's father, now a very rich man, had been an embezzler in his youth. He had stolen $10,000, and on this he had built his fortune. "You know what the priest told him?" said Romero to Father Perez.

Of course Father Perez knew. There was only one thing a priest could tell the dying man. He had to restore the money.

"The man from whom my father took that money is here in Los Angeles," said Romero. "That I know, and I have the name of an agent who will act for me. He will see that the money is returned to the man my father injured. He will do it quietly, so there is no disgrace. But I cannot find him. I went to the address which my father gave me and he is not there."

"And the man from whom your father took the money?" asked Father Perez.

"I cannot find him either. But I do not wish to see him. I wish to have someone act for me. I cannot see this man. I am not well myself." Senor Romero put his hand to his stomach and said, "Ulcera!"

"He got a stomach ulcer?" asked Kelly.

Father Perez nodded.

"It is very painful," said Romero.

Father Perez was sympathetic, and he was also helpful. He suggested that Senor Romero consult the telephone directories for the addresses of the injured man and the agent whom his father had suggested. He even led Senor Romero to the directories near the public telephone in the hospital corridor. He could not, however, find the name of the suggested agent, or the name of the man who had been bilked of $10,000. To his alarm, Senor Romero displayed complete bewilderment as to what to do next. He also took out a handsome wallet and displayed quantities of money. "It is the ten thousand, Padre," said Romero. "What am I to do? I cannot go back to my father and tell him that I have failed. I must restore the money. And there is more. There is a fee for the agent. Or I must see that the money is given to a charity. That is what the priest said."

Mr. Kelly erupted into the hospital corridor at that point, and his eyes lighted on the wad of bills. "What's up?" he demanded. "What's he doing?"

"He needs a commissionary to handle this money for him," explained the priest.

"It must be someone of great honor," said the South American. He spoke in English now. "It is an affair of trust. I cannot remain here. I am ill. I am in pain. I must return to my home. Only I must find this commissionary first."

"Oh?" said Kelly. "You want somebody who's trustworthy? What's the matter with Father Perez here?"

"The priest?" Senor Romero stared at Father Perez. "But a priest is not a man of business."

"Sure he is," Kelly contradicted him. "All priests are businessmen. They have to be. You know, they have to run their parishes and pay the janitors and build schools and raise money."

Senor Romero looked hopeful. "There is a fee for the agent," he reminded Father Perez. "If you would do it, Father? You understand what is involved. Only...only are you really a man of business? I must assure my father that I have entrusted the money to someone who will handle it well."

Father Perez did not really wish to become involved in the

matter, and he felt a pang of anxiety at the thought of the responsibility of handling $10,000 belonging to someone else. But then he thought proudly of his fiesta, and of the large sum now in his building fund. "I am a man of business," he said. He still had the receipted deposit slip from the bank in his pocket, and now he produced it to show Senor Romero that only this morning he had put $10,173 into the bank.

Romero squinted at the thing. "This little piece of paper means that you have more than $10,000 which you can administrate?"

Father Perez nodded.

"You can draw this money on demand?" asked Romero.

"Of course he can," said Mr. Kelly. "It's his parish and he gets to handle the money."

Senor Romero shook his head. "I do not understand about this paper," he said. "I wish to see the money. I wish to assure my father that I have trusted his money to a man who is accustomed to handle money in this amount."

"He's a hard guy to convince, Father," said Kelly.

"I must know that the matter is in good hands," insisted the man from Caracas.

"What do you say, Father?" asked Kelly. "You going to draw out the ten thousand and show it to our skeptical friend?"

Father Perez announced that he was not going to draw out the proceeds of his fiesta.

"Look, Mr. Romero," said Kelly reasonably, "suppose Father got $5,000 and showed it to you. Would that convince you?"

Senor Romero looked doubtful.

Kelly looked at his watch. "We've got half an hour," he told the priest. "My sister won't be back in her room for half an hour at least — maybe longer."

Father Perez pondered on Senor Romero's pain, and his anxiety to do the proper thing. And for a fleeting instant he considered the fee which was to be paid to the commissionary. It might possibly be added to the building fund. There would be no risk, really. Anyone in his parish — anyone who knew of the fiesta — would think that he had made a deposit if they saw him leave the bank. No one would suspect that he had withdrawn money.

"You want to get the money?" asked Mr. Kelly. "I'll stay here and keep Mr. Romero company. He looks like he's hurting."

Romero moaned a small, heart-rending moan. It moved Father Perez. It moved him out to the parking lot and over to the bank, where he withdrew $5,000 from his building fund. He hurried back to the hospital, where he found Mr. Kelly and Senor Romero in the coffee shop. Romero was attempting to soothe his pain with a milk shake.

Father Perez sat down across from Romero. He took the envelope with $5,000 from his pocket, opened it slightly, and riffled through the bills so that Romero could see them.

"Ah!" said the man from Caracas.

"Don't flash that around!" warned Kelly.

Senor Romero unfolded a handkerchief and spread it on the table. He then opened his handsome wallet, took out a veritable mountain of bills and a small piece of paper and put these down on the handkerchief. "Here is $10,000," he said, "and on this paper is written the name of the man who is to receive the money. Also, there is $500 as a fee for the commissionary. That is for you."

Then, almost as an afterthought, he took the bank envelope from the priest and put that on top of the thousands of dollars piled on the handkerchief. "You will take care of everything," he said, and began to fold the money into the handkerchief.

"Here comes the waitress, you imbecile!" snapped Kelly.

Romero jumped, looked around at the weary girl who was approaching to see if he wanted another milk shake, and scooped the handkerchief, money and all, onto his lap and out of sight. He then informed the girl that he wanted nothing more. His business was finished.

When the waitress departed, Romero replaced the handerchief on the table, tied all four ends so that it made a neat bundle and handed it to Father Perez. "You will take care?" he asked.

"I will take good care," promised the priest.

Romero nodded. "My father will be pleased," he said. "I go now to my hotel, where I have my ticket for the plane."

He stood up and started for the door. Halfway there he stopped and leaned on a table.

Kelly jumped up and hurried to him. "How are you going to get to the hotel?" he asked.

"I take a taxicab," said the South American.

"Where you ought to go is upstairs to the ulcer ward, if they have one," advised Kelly.

Romero shook his head. "I must return to my home."

"Father, I'll make sure he gets a cab," said Kelly to the priest. "The cabby'll take it from there. They're good at this kind of thing. You wait a second and I'll be right back."

Father Perez nodded. Kelly and the South American went out into the corridor, with Romero leaning weakly on Kelly.

Mr. Kelly did not return. And when Father Perez became uneasy and repaired to the men's room off the hospital corridor, he opened the handkerchief and found that he did not have his own $5,000, or Mr. Romero's $10,000 or the $500 fee for the agent. He had a handkerchief and a pile of paper. He knew that he would be visiting the chancery office, and that the visit would not be pleasant.

Father Perez, a kind and honest man, had been the victim of a bunco scheme which is call the charity switch.

Any Fairly Substantial Citizen Can Be Taken in by the Charity Switch; Priests Are Not the Only Victims. A well-dressed person might be approached on the street by a bewildered foreigner searching for a certain person. The victim and the bewildered foreigner then may be approached by a second con man who seems to wander along by accident and who is then drawn into the conversation. The second con man isn't able to locate the man from whom the first con's daddy filched that huge sum of money all those years ago, but he lingers on the scene being vaguely helpful. He's sorry that the visitor from a foreign shore is feeling so poorly that he must return home immediately — and the foreigner is always feeling poorly. One way or another, he will urge that the foreign guest trust the victim, who seems like an honest and also substantial person. He will also support the demand of the foreign guest that the victim display money to show his good faith and demonstrate his responsibility.

Once the victim draws money out of his bank, it is put into an envelope, a handkerchief or a purse along with the money displayed by the con man. At this point, the second con man creates some diversion, such as the approach of the waitress in the hospital coffee shop. The money is swept out of sight for a moment. In that moment, the envelope, handkerchief or purse containing the real money disappears forever from the victim's sight. The handkerchief in the hospital coffee shop was switched for another which had been prepared in advance. The two con men depart together, one promising the other assistance in getting to his hotel or his plane.

Father Perez did have an unpleasant time in the offices of the Archdiocese of Los Angeles when he confessed that his building fund was $5,000 short. The officials at the chancery office were exceedingly wroth, and since Father Perez' church was in Los Angeles County, rather than the City of Los Angeles, and since the fraud had occurred in county territory, there was a hot telephone call to the county sheriff's office.

There was also a visit by Father Perez to the sheriff's bunco division. Father Perez went through the mug books and did not find any photograph which resembled Senor Romero or Mr. Kelly. One of the sheriff's men considered it likely that Romero and Kelly might continue their act in the area, possibly with other parish priests who could have a few thousand tucked into the building fund or the school fund or some other fund.

The sheriff's man called the Los Angeles Police Department, which has jurisdiction within the city limits. By an absolutely weird coincidence, two men answering to the descriptions given by Father Perez had just had an interesting conversation with Father James O'Boyle in the coffee shop of Hollywood Presbyterian Hospital, where Father O'Boyle had gone to shrive the soul of one man's sister — a woman long separated from her church. Father O'Boyle had found the conversation so interesting that he had hurried to his bank. From there he had called the police.

The Los Angeles Police knew at least as much about the charity switch as anyone and had been prepared to have Father O'Boyle return to the hospital with the faith money. The instant the switch was made, the police planned to nab the two confidence men. As it turned out, this wasn't necessary. Father Perez saved his colleague the trouble of withdrawing money from his school fund. He identified thecons.

There are other ways in which strangers supposedly in need of help can separate well-intentioned citizens from their cash.

THE JAMAICAN SWINDLE IS A PLAY ON PATRIOTISM. This particular flim-flam game usually involves a sailor fresh off a boat. It originated in port cities along the Atlantic coast; and the sailor often claimed to be from the West Indies, hence the name Jamaican swindle.

The victim of the Jamaican swindle is not likely to be a very prosperous businessman or a member of the clergy. Roosevelt Tompkins, a thirty-two-year-old male Negro, a warehouseman, was caught off guard by a pair of bunco men operating the Jamaican swindle.

Tompkins was having a quiet drink in a bar after work when he was approached by a dark-skinned man who claimed to be off a ship from Jamaica. The seaman said he had never been in the United States before and he was troubled because he was carrying an undisclosed amount of cash. He claimed that the ship's captain had warned him never to deposit money in "the white man's bank" because such a deposit is a "one-way deal" and blacks cannot draw their money out again.

Tompkins stoutly declared that anyone with money in a bank can draw it out any time.

The sailor looked doubtful.

A second sailor arrived and joined in the conversation. In his opinion, the money could not be withdrawn by a black.

Tompkins offered to prove that indeed he could draw money out of the bank. The next day one of the sailors went with him to the bank and watched him take money from his savings account. Tompkins and the sailor then went to a small hotel nearby to show the cash to the first sailor, who was supposedly in the hotel sleeping off the grog he had absorbed the night before. In front of the hotel, Tompkins gave $750 in cash to the second sailor, who went into the place, supposedly to display the cash to his hungover friend.

Tompkins never saw either sailor again.

Roosevelt Tompkins had absolutely nothing to gain by withdrawing money from his bank. He only wanted to show that rumors about the United States were groundless. His willingness to stand up for his country cost him almost every dollar he had saved over a period of four years.

Tompkins' misfortune is not unusual. In New Orleans, a thirty-eight-year-old truck driver was approached in a cafeteria by two men who said they were off a ship. One man offered to bet that the truck driver could not take money out of a bank. The driver went to the bank and withdrew money, accompanied by one of the supposed seamen. The seaman put the money into an envelope and returned to the cafeteria, where he displayed the envelope to his confederate. So the truck driver won his bet, except that the con men returned to him an envelope that was supposed to contain his money, plus the amount of the bet. The envelope contained only newspaper clippings.

SOMETIMES, AS IN THE SPANISH PRISONER SWINDLE, THE AILING ALIEN ISN'T EVEN ON THE SCENE. The Spanish prisoner swindle dates back to the days when city slickers sold gold bricks to country bumpkins, and it has been exposed in the press hundreds of times, but it is still used occasionally.

And it still works.

The good Samaritan who is taken in by this bunco game is usually a man with an eye for a pretty girl, a generous heart, and a yearning for adventure.

One of the con artists is a pretty girl.

The second con artist is a man who poses as her uncle.

The good Samaritan meets the pretty girl and their friendship grows and blossoms, and before long there are confidences and kisses and, since the good Samaritan is a kindly and sensitive person, he notices that the girl is troubled. Indeed she is troubled. Her father is being held in jail in some South American country. Any South American country which has recently undergone a political upheaval will do. It will take thousands of dollars to bail him out or buy his escape or ransom him, and the girl does not have the money. Neither does the uncle. They are desperate.

If the good Samaritan is truly pure of heart, he may come up with the cash immediately.

He may need some prodding. He may be informed that the father, and only that distant, imprisoned father, knows the location of a buried treasure (or, perhaps, the number of a private Swiss bank account).

And, if the girl is being nice to the good Samaritan now, think how absolutely marvelous she will be once her father is rescued. And how grateful will be the ransomed parent.

The good Samaritan will provide the needed cash. He may even drive his sweetheart and her uncle to the airport, so that they can fly to South America and retrieve the father.

Once they are aboard the plane, they will be seen no more.

It is difficult to help a bred-in-the-bone good Samaritan. He wants to believe in his fellow man, in God and his country, in pretty girls and true repentance, and all of those nice things. Occasionally the bunco cop gets a break in the form of someone like Father O'Boyle, who might have had his eyes on the stars, but who also had his feet on the ground and who had the good sense to call the police when someone suggested that he take money out of the bank to show that he was responsible.

When they get that kind of a break, the bunco cops have to move fast to save other good Samaritans down the line. In the case of Father Perez and Father O'Boyle, the police and the sheriff's men were weak with relief that Father O'Boyle did *not* have to withdraw his money and let the con artists get their hands on it even for a second. "They were nervous as hell," recalls one cop. "They were going to jump in the second the cons handed that handkerchief back to the priest. Those guys can move like smoke, and they were afraid that somehow, someway, once they got the dough, they'd beat it."

Chapter 5

THE FIX-IT MEN

THE average homeowner spends several hundred dollars a year maintaining or improving his dwelling. A shocking percentage of this money goes to the flim-flam man who *does* perform a service. The service is not what is represented to the homeowner, but this particular variety of con artist (and the terrible Williamson clan is the most famous of all) works a bit harder than the pigeon drop team or the ring of "bank examiners."

Bradley Housemann, seventy-one years old and retired, encountered a couple of these "workmen" one afternoon when he was painting the trim around the front door of his house in a suburb of Buffalo. The suburb was not one of the more affluent, and Mr. Housemann's home needed paint. It also needed a new roof.

A pair of workmen who claimed to be from the Acme Roofing Company stopped their pickup truck in front of the house, and the driver of the truck got out and approached Mr. Housemann and squinted at the roof.

"That's in pretty bad shape," said the man to Housemann.

Housemann admitted that the roof was not what it once had been; he worried about the roof sometimes, since it rains a great deal in Buffalo.

The workman from the truck then confided to Housemann that he and his partner had just finished a roofing job two blocks away. They had oil left over from the job, and could waterproof Housemann's roof for only a fraction of the usual cost since the oil was already paid for.

"We don't need to return that oil to Acme," was the way the con man put it. "We can fix your roof, make a couple of extra bucks for ourselves, and save you some dough. The boss will never be the wiser."

Housemann hesitated. He almost decided against accepting

this money-saving offer. But, while he pondered on it, the two roofers put together extension ladders from their truck, hauled out cans of oil and a spray gun, and proceeded to oil the roof. They worked quickly, and within the hour informed Housemann that his roof was waterproof, that the job would be good for at least twenty years, and that he owed them $150.

Mr. Housemann did not have $150, but he felt by this time that he was totally compromised. He had allowed the men to put oil which was either the property of "the boss" or of the homeowner three blocks away, onto his roof. He wrote a check to the con men and they drove off.

Two days later it did rain. The oil was washed off Housemann's roof, staining the sides of his home and killing off large patches of his lawn.

Only then did Housemann attempt to contact the roofing company. He learned that the company had no employees answering the description given by Housemann, and there had not been a roofing job in Housemann's neighborhood.

The owner of the roofing company was an honest businessman, and he was outraged that someone was using the name of his firm as a cover for a swindle. He insisted that Housemann call the police, which Housemann did. Because of the delay in reporting the swindle, the two "roofers" were never apprehended. Housemann did discover that they had cashed his check at his bank on the same day he wrote it. He had made the check payable to Ned Parker, the name given to him by one of the cons, and "Parker" had used a driver's license as identification. A check with the state revealed that the license was fictitious.

ELDERLY PEOPLE ARE OFTEN THE VICTIMS OF THIS FRAUD. Bradley Housemann, at seventy-one was still mentally alert — alert enough to know that he had not acted quite honorably in accepting roofing material from men who did not really own that material.

Many elderly people are senile to a degree, or lonely and defenseless.

One seventy-five-year-old man was pulling weeds out of his front lawn when he was approached by a pair of scammers. The pitch? "We've been putting in a new lawn down the street and have fertilizer left over. We hate to dump it or tote it all the way back to the supply yard. We can spread it on your lawn for almost nothing."

The homeowner told the men to go ahead, and they did. Twenty minutes later they were finished with the job, and they demanded $200. When the victim protested, the two con men became abusive. One of them actually struck him. A neighbor who lived across the street witnessed the scene and called the police.

The police arrived promptly and apprehended the two suspects, who were booked for assault and battery. They forfeited bail and left the area.

Later inspection proved that the "fertilizer" which had been spread on the victim's law was 96 percent sawdust and 4 percent steer manure. It had cost the scammers about three dollars; and if it had not been for the kindly neighbor, they might have forced the victim to pay them $200 for the stuff.

THERE IS ALMOST NO LIMIT TO THE "SERVICES" WHICH THE BUNCO ARTISTS CAN OFFER. One victim was approached by two men who offered to inspect his home for termites, borers, dry rot, or any of the other afflictions which can beset a house. Since the inspections was free, the victim told them to go ahead. One man crawled under the house and emerged very shortly holding three snakes. The victim was informed that there was a nest of snakes under the house. The "inspectors" offered to rid the place of snakes by sealing the house and pumping a special gas into it. The victim consented to this, and the "inspectors" filled his home with a vile-smelling gas which promptly permeated all the furniture and clothing. They collected $200 from the victim and disappeared. It cost the victim more than $100 to have his furniture and clothing cleaned and his house fumigated. The fumigator who did the work informed him that there were no snakes under the house, and there had never been snakes under the house. The reptiles had been carried in by one of the "inspectors."

Con artists will spread oil on asphalt driveways at a cut price — and not a small price — and hapless homeowners will see the oil wash away the first time it rains, or the first time the lawn is watered.

Free inspections of oil burners are another come-on. The homeowner who lets an unknown and unsummoned "inspector" into the basement to check the safety and efficiency of the heating system will probably find himself paying large amounts of money for unneeded repairs — or perhaps even putting a down payment on a new oil burner.

One woman in Indiana was approached by "inspectors" who asked if they could examine the foundation of her bungalow. She consented to this, and soon the con men reported that, "This Japanese mortar mouse was caught eating the concrete around your house foundations." The woman authorized the con men to exterminate any Japanese mortar mice which might be lurking on her property and almost immediately had second thoughts. She had friends at the courthouse in her county. She called those friends, and the "inspectors" were apprehended, with their "Japanese mortar mouse," three blocks from the woman's home.

NOT ALL CON MEN WORKING THE HOME REPAIRS SWINDLES OPERATE ON A HIT-AND-RUN BASIS. Some maintain offices and manage to remain in business for long periods. They always deliver a product or a service, but what they offer is overpriced and often of shoddy manufacture.

These swindlers do not work from street corners; they use the telephone for the initial contact and manage to be invited to the victim's home.

Ernesto and Maria Torres encountered a pair of bunco artists of the more stable kind.

The Torres couple lived in Tahitian Terrace, a tract of modest homes on the coastal flats of Oxnard, California. They had come from Mexico and were becoming typical Americans as rapidly as possible — eager to do the proper thing and obey all the laws.

It was afternoon and Maria Torres was alone when she received a telephone call. The caller sounded young, female, friendly, and she told Mrs. Torres that she was calling from the water company.

"We're making a survey of the water in the county," said the woman on the telephone. "We would like permission to send two men to your house to examine the water. Do you object if we do this?"

Mrs. Torres did not object. She thought it was a fine thing if the officials of the county were concerned that the water be okay.

"When will your husband be home?" asked the caller.

"Mi esposo?" said Mrs. Torres.

"Yes, your husband. We prefer to talk to both of you. Will he be home tonight?"

"Tonight? Yes. He is home at night."

"May the men come this evening, then?" asked the woman from the water company.

Maria Torres agreed that the men could come that evening, and that eight o'clock would be a convenient time.

At three minutes before eight that night, the doorbell rang. Maria Torres opened the door and saw two men on the small porch. One wore overalls and had dirt under his fingernails and the other was conservatively dressed in a business suit and carried a black attaché case.

The men introduced themselves. The man with overalls was Schulte, and the other man was Hanson. Hanson displayed identification — an official-looking document in a leather folder. The men then took seats in the little living room and delivered a short lecture on water to Ernesto and Maria Torres.

"As you know," said Mr. Hanson, "there are many kinds of water. Some is fresh, very pure. Other water has minerals and other impurities."

Ernesto Torres understood this and he nodded.

"From time to time, we like to check the quality of the water that is being delivered to users in the area. May we examine *your* water?"

But of course they could. They did. They went into Maria Torres' kitchen and Mr. Hanson opened his attaché case, which was filled with test tubes, vials, jars of liquids. Hanson filled a test tube with water from the kitchen tap. He held it up to the light and decided that it looked fine — but also that looks could be deceiving. He then put the test tube of water in a rack built into his attaché case and added to it liquid from a glass vial.

A moment later, particles formed in the test tube and settled to the bottom.

Mr. Hanson scowled.

Mr. Schulte glared at the test tube and said, "Sludge! Awful!"

Hanson then gave the test tube to Ernesto Torres so that he

could see for himself. "To think that that crud is going into your stomachs!" he exclaimed.

Maria Torres happened to be quite pregnant at the time, and this fact had not escaped Hanson's notice. "You don't realize what this gunk can do to the human body," he said. "I've got records back at the office which prove this sludge can lead to TB, cancer, gallstones and ..." He lowered his voice. "It can lead to pregnancy problems," he said. "Water that isn't pure can make an unborn baby ... well, sick!"

There was more then; more testing of the water, checking of pipes under the sink, out in the garage, under the hot water heater. Finally there was the test of the purifier, a little cylinder which Hanson clipped onto a test tube. When the test tube was filled with tap water which had been run through the cylinder, the results were perfect. No sediment. No sludge.

"Tastes wonderful, doesn't it?" said Hanson. "Tastes like water *should* taste. No minerals or other unhealthy impurities."

Ernesto and Maria Torres sipped and agreed that the water was good.

It was. It had been filtered through an ordinary purifier, smaller than usual but with the same salts contained in the large commercial units.

"Would you like to have water like that in your house?" Hanson asked.

Ernesto Torres would like that very much, but he winced when he learned that a water purifier would cost him $650.

"Oh?" said Hanson. "Of course, maybe you're immune to disease. And your baby will probably be born okay anyway."

Both Ernesto and Maria Torres were terribly distressed.

"If you would like to guarantee the health of your wife and your unborn child," said Hanson, "then the purifier is not expensive."

Ten minutes later, Hanson and Schulte left the Torres home, and Maria and Ernesto Torres had signed a contract to purchase a rebuilt water softener they didn't need at a price only three times the normal price for a new one.

The next morning, Mr. Hanson picked up the telephone, dialed a finance company in Los Angeles, and arranged to sell the Torres' contract for a mere $550.

That might have been the end of it, except for large payments by Ernesto Torres to the fiannce company, but the next day, Torres discussed the matter with his boss. The boss knew that the water company does not sell water softeners, that water softeners do not cost $650, and that there was nothing in the Oxnard water which would cause harm to Maria's child.

By five o'clock that afternoon, the Oxnard police had heard about the Torres case. There is nothing illegal about selling water softeners, but the inflated cost and the method of selling were suspicious. An investigative unit set to work studying computer print-outs from Washington to see if similar operations had been working and who was running them. Since they suspected a boiler room operation (a rented store or office with a bank of telephones from which salesmen can make their initial contacts), they contacted the telephone company to find out if anyone had ordered a number of telephones in recent weeks. They also called the water company to see if complaints had come in from customers who were distressed by the fact that they had "dirty water."

The police were able to locate other victims. These victims had not complained because they did not know they had been taken. Hanson and Schulte were only two of a ring of scammers who specialized in bilking newly-arrived Americans. There were a couple of women in the group who staffed the boiler room. They went through the telephone directory looking for names of people who might be from Mexico. The salesmen followed up on the telephone contacts and, as witnesses were interviewed, the pattern became clear. The cons were using scare words such as cancer, TB and pregnancy to frighten the prospective customers into signing up. If this did not work, the salesman would tell the newcomer that water purifiers were part of the American way of life. The salesman could usually make the new citizen feel guilty about not having a water softener.

The water softeners were delivered and installed, but it was plain that the cons intended to defraud their Mexican-American customers. They lied, and lied consistently.

The district attorney's office was able to bring suit against the frauds. Unfortunately, in most cases they were not able to recover the money from the customers who had been swindled or to relieve those customers of the responsibility of paying $650 for the water purifiers. They were, however, able to put the scammers out of business — in that area.

SOMETIMES THE FIX-IT FRAUDS CAN CONTINUE TO OPERATE. One homeowner, Victor Savella, a twenty-nine-year-old supermarket manager, was visited at home by a salesman for aluminum siding. The salesman showed Savella brochures and fact sheets showing how aluminum siding saved on fuel bills, reflected heat for more comfort in the summer, and eliminated the need for costly paint jobs on a home. Savella did not bother to check with local firms supplying aluminum siding; he did not have a chance to check, since the salesman's visit occurred at night, when established contractors are closed, and the salesman pressured him to sign a contract immediately. He purchased the siding for his house for $6,150. Later he learned that the job had been given to a local company for $1,000. In fact, a neighbor was contracted to do the work. However, the contract was legal and Savella had to pay the full $6,150.

IT IS NOT ALWAYS POSSIBLE TO PROTECT PEOPLE FROM THE FIX-IT MEN BUT GOOD RAPPORT BETWEEN LAW ENFORCEMENT AGENCIES AND THE COMMUNITY CAN HELP. In some states, the consumer who has second thoughts about a contract he has signed has two or three days in which to change his mind; he can back out. In some states he is stuck.

In all states he should feel free to check with his local police department when a salesman seems a bit out of line. A sergeant taking a call in the bunco department may not be able to say outright that a salesman is a con artist, but he can advise caution — and a waiting period — if any of the following pitches have been used:

1. "We are giving you a special rate on this aluminum siding (brick patio, swimming pool, roof) because we believe that your home will be a showcase for our product. You will actually be helping us to sell aluminum siding (brick patios, swimming pools)."

2. "Who was the first president of the United States? U.S. Grant? Well, that's close enough. We would like to have on our salesmen call on you..."

3. "Yes, the special we advertised is only $129, but you can see that it isn't the quality you're accustomed to. Now, for only $200 more..." This particular ploy is called "bait and switch" and is widely used by the fix-it men and also by appliance salesmen. A "special" is offered at a ridiculously low price. This enables the salesman to get the foot in the door — or the customer into his shop. Once the contact has been made, the customer will be sold off the low-priced "special" and convinced that he can't get along without the more expensive appliance or service.
4. "You'll be safeguarding your health and the health of your family."
5. "It will cost you less than a pack of cigarettes a day." If a homeowner is signing a contract that will run for three years, he is signing for several hundred dollars.
6. "My company pays me ten dollars for each demonstration I make, so you'll be doing me a favor if you let me show you our..." This is another ploy which enables the salesman to get in the door.
7. "It will cost you nothing," or "This is absolutely free, but..."

In some areas there are organizations such as the Los Angeles Bureau of Consumer Affairs, and callers can be advised to contact these offices. In all cases, the bunco cop should listen carefully and take the reports — and see if perhaps that pattern indicating intent to defraud appears as reports accumulated.

Of course, if a homeowner calls in to question the credentials of a pair of workmen who have offered a cut-rate on a job because the materials have already been paid for by another customer, it is not necessary to wait or ponder. Send a squad car to the scene immediately. The terrible Williamsons are probably back in town.

Chapter 6

PYRAMIDS HAVE TO TOUCH GROUND

In the 1940s there were pyramid parties, and a few people made lots of money and a lot of people made nothing at all. The reason that so many people made nothing at all is that pyramid clubs — or sales schemes or letters — cannot possibly continue for more than a limited time.

THE CHAIN LETTER IS PROBABLY THE OLDEST AND MOST FAMILIAR OF THE PYRAMID SCHEMES. Chain letters requesting money are illegal, but few adults who possess a mailing address haven't received at least one. A typical chain letter reads about as follows:

> Do not throw this letter away. Do not break the chain.
> Captain Kenneth Bickerson broke the chain, and within five days he lost $1,000,000 on the stock market.
> Mrs. Janet Mullins did not break the chain, and in two weeks she received $57,000.
> You can receive more than $60,000 within two weeks if you keep this letter going. Send one dollar to the person whose name is at the top of the list below. Then make four copies of this letter. Remove the name and address of the person who is at the top of the list and add your name and address to the bottom of the list.
> Send the letter on to four friends. Within two weeks, get ready to sit back and count your money.

At the bottom of such a letter, the names and addresses of perhaps eight people appear. The name at the bottom of the list is usually the name of some friend of the recipient.

Let us say that the recipient is Mrs. A., and she does not wish to disappoint her friend, who has sent her this letter. Also, she believes that adding her name to the bottom of the list and forwarding copies of the letter to four friends may be an easy way to make a heap of money. Perhaps Mrs. A. sits down with a pencil and paper and figures it out. She feels that it is certainly possible to make more than $60,000, provided no one breaks the chain.

She will send the letter to four friends.

The four friends will each send the letter to four friends, thus involving sixteen people in addition to the four friends in addition to Mrs. A — a total of twenty-one.

The sixteen new recipients forward the letter, each to four people, bringing sixty-four more into the pyramid — eighty-five people.

At the next step, the sixty-four members of the pyramid would send on the letter to 256 new prospects — 341 people.

If the 256 new prospects all continued the chain, another 1,024 people would be contacted, and the membership in the pyramid would be 1,365.

At the sixth step from Mrs. A., if the chain remained unbroken, 1,024 people would have to contact 4,096 people, and there would be 5,461 hopefuls in the pyramid.

At step seven, the progression would be 4,096 x 4 = 16,384. A total of 21,845 people would have received letters.

Step eight? 16,384 x 4 = 65,536 + 21,845 = 87,381.

Step nine? 65,536 x 4 = 262,144

At this step, Mrs. A. should, theoretically, have heaps and piles and mountains of dollar bills. Even if one or two surly souls have *not* forwarded their letters, she should have thousands and thousands. She will not, however, because for a chain letter to go through nine steps, a total of more than 300,000 people would have to be contacted.

While it is remotely possible that this many recipients could be involved, it isn't at all likely. The chain letter fails for all except the ones who start the entire process.

They fail because chain letters which solicit money are illegal, and the chain will be broken. People will throw the letters away or turn them in to a postal inspector or return them to the sender with a polite note.

Also, they fail because there are not enough people in the world. If Mrs. A. carries her arithmetic a bit further, she will realize that if the chain goes unbroken through ten steps, more than a million people would have to be contacted.

At step eleven, an additional four million would be the recipients, and at step twelve the number jumps to sixteen million.

Soon the entire population of the United States would be used up, and letters would be opened in far-off Cambodia, Thailand, and Argentina.

The pyramid would have touched ground.

The pyramid chain letter is a minor bunk, and the mails are not always used in this sort of scheme. The message can be forwarded by telephone. The old pyramid parties were simple affairs where people were invited to come, have a cup of coffee, give a dollar to the person whose name was at the top of the list and add their own names to the bottom of the list. The game can be played with whiskey, savings bonds, stock certificates — anything of value.

The games do not last long because of the shortage of people, and the people who originate the schemes often cannot be prosecuted because their names are lost as the chain progresses. As long as the amount involved is only a dollar or a bottle of whiskey, no one is too badly hurt. There are, however, pyramid schemes in which the victims are very badly hurt.

AT FIRST GLANCE, THE REFERRAL SALES SCHEME DOESN'T LOOK LIKE A PYRAMID. At first glance, the referral sales scheme looks like a chance for the consumer to get something he'd like at a price which anyone can afford — nothing, or perhaps a few dollars down and then monthly payments of nothing for two years.

Appliances, encyclopedias and luxurious items such as home intercom systems have been sold in this way.

A friend of one of the authors, whom we will call Mrs. Johnson, was the victim of a ring of bunco artists who peddled home intercom systems.

Mrs. Johnson, a young matron, lived in a sprawling ranch-style home and had most of the things young matrons enjoy. She had a dishwasher, a washing machine, a dryer, wall-to-wall carpeting, and her own car. She also had a husband whose salary barely stretched to cover the payments on these gadgets, and she had two small children who wandered off to far corners of the house and quietly got into mischief.

One afternoon Mrs. Johnson received a telephone call from an acquaintance, Ann Barker. Mrs. Johnson had known Ann for several years, but didn't see her often. Ann lived on the far side of town, and it wasn't easy to arrange baby-sitters except for special occasions.

Ann had a strange request. Would Mrs. Johnson allow a representative of the Instant Sound Service Company to call on her and her husband?

"What for?" asked Mrs. Johnson.

"Well, he's got this great system," said Ann Barker. "You'd like it, with that big house. Besides, you'd be doing me a favor. I told him I'd get in touch with you."

Everyone likes to do a friend a favor, and it wouldn't cost anything to listen.

The salesman, Fred Atkins, telephoned the next day, introduced himself as Ann Barker's contact, and set a time when he could call on Mrs. Johnson and her husband.

Mr. Johnson was greatly on his guard that evening when he learned that a representative of a firm called Instant Sound Service was going to call. He was already paying on too many gadgets, and a sound service had the ring of gadget about it.

At 8:30, after the children were in bed, Fred Atkins appeared at the door with an attache case bulging with brochures on his product. He looked around the Johnsons' living room with interest, grinned and went into his pitch. He could install an intercom system in the house that would make life simpler, easier and safer for all who dwelt there. With his system, Mrs. Johnson could stand in the kitchen in the morning, frying eggs, and chat with Mr. Johnson while he shaved way off there in the bathroom. More important, Mrs. Johnson could inform Mr. Johnson when the eggs were done. She wouldn't have to shout, and she wouldn't have to race the length of the house.

The system would also be an electronic baby-sitter for the children. The Johnsons could leave the receiver on in Karen's room and they would hear her if she got up in the night and tried to float toys in the toilet. With the system Mrs. Johnson could listen in on Jeffrey, who liked to go off by himself and take things apart.

And, with the system, they could find out who was at the front door without leaving their walled-in patio. The unwelcome or dangerous caller could be kept out without the risk of a face-to-face confrontation. Since Mr. Johnson sometimes traveled in connection with his work, this safety factor was most important.

To Mr. Johnson, the cost of the system was important. "We can't do it," he said. "I'm already mortgaged to the ears."

"I was getting to that," announced Fred Atkins. "It will cost you practically nothing to have our system installed in your house."

"Exactly how much is practically nothing?" demanded Mr. Johnson.

Atkins began figuring. The down payment would be only $57.50, and the monthly payments would be in the neighborhood of $33.75, and the total price, including interest would be $630.00.

"But I don't anticipate that you'll have to make any monthly payments," said Atkins. "We've had customers who've paid for their intercoms without any cost to themselves within three or four months."

Fred Atkins then explained how the Johnsons could have the superlative intercom system without making any installment payments. They could simply furnish him with the names of people who might also desire an intercom. Atkins would contact these people. For every system he sold, he would pay the Johnsons a commission of thirty dollars, which would be applied against the cost of the system.

"Ann Barker," said Mrs. Johnson quickly. "Did she buy an intercom system from you?"

"It was installed in her home last week," said Atkins. "She's very happy with it, and of course thirty dollars of the $57.50 which you put down on your system will go to the Barkers as their commission, since Mrs. Barker referred me to you."

"My word!" said Mrs. Johnson.

"I want to see the sales contract," said Mr. Johnson.

Atkins gladly showed Mr. Johnson the standard sales contract of the Instant Sound Service. Mr. Johnson read all the fine print twice over, and it was true. For every sale Atkins made as a result of a referral, the Johnsons would receive a commission of thirty dollars to be applied toward the cost of their own intercom.

Mr. Johnson frowned and began figuring. Most of his friends lived in sprawling, spread-out homes. Most of his associates traveled in connection with their work. If Atkins only sold one or two systems a month, the cost of the intercom would be paid off without pain or strain.

The Johnsons signed for an intercom, and Mr. Johnson made out a check for $57.50 as a down payment. He was sure it would be the last check he would have to write to Instant Sound Service.

Ann Barker called the next day. Atkins had been in touch with her to inform her that the Johnsons had taken an intercom and that thirty dollars would be applied against her account with Instant Sound Service. She was pleased. The Johnsons were the first people she had referred to Instant Sound who had signed for the system.

They were also the last. Mrs. Barker made no more successful referrals. She and her husband paid more than $600 for their intercom system. As for the Johnsons, not one of their referrals panned out. They paid the full price, plus interest, for a system which could have been installed in their home for less than $400 if they had gone to any legitimate technician.

The Johnsons and the Barkers had gotten involved in a pyramid game, and a very difficult pyramid game. More than a dollar was involved, and since few people really *need* an intercom system, they ran out of prospects almost immediately.

If Mr. Johnson had taken time to think the matter through, he would have realized that he would have to furnish Atkins with twenty successful referrals to pay the balance due on his contract. It would be madness to think that Atkins would not propose the same referral plan to the prospects supplied by Mr. Johnson. If each had an intercom installed, each would in turn have to give Atkins eighteen or twenty names, and Atkins would be calling upon hundreds of prospects. The pyramid would quickly broaden and Instant Sound Service would be installing their systems in thousands of homes.

Assuming the scheme would work, which it could not, Instant Sound Service would go on endlessly installing intercoms for $57.50 down and returning thirty dollars to the customer who made the referral, then following up more referrals and returning yet more money to the customer; and Instant Sound Service would go broke because, in the end, no one would pay more than $27.50 for a sound system.

But Instant Sound Service did make money because the owners

of the firm knew that what they were pushing was a pyramid game and that pyramid games don't work. The victims could not possibly make enough successful referrals, and the victims had to pay.

Referral sales schemes are all pyramid games. They are outlawed in some states and have come to the attention of the United States Department of Justice and, where the mails are used, of the postal authorities.

NOT ALL PYRAMID OPERATIONS INVOLVE ANYTHING AS SIMPLE AS AN INTERCOM SYSTEM. SOME ARE FRANCHISE OPERATIONS, IN WHICH THE VICTIMS ARE ENCOURAGED TO "GO INTO BUSINESS" OR "EARN AN EXTRA $500 A MONTH WORKING PART-TIME." The victim is usually enticed into a franchise scheme when he or she receives an invitation to an "opportunity meeting." The victim is not told what the opportunity is unless he goes to the meeting. If he takes the bait and attends the meeting, he will find himself being enthusiastically greeted by the management of the XYZ Soap Company (or possibly the management of a firm that sells cosmetics or shoe polish or mending tape or kitchen knives). The prospect may be told that he or she can make a modest amount, such as $500 a month, selling the company's product from door to door. The initial investment will be modest. Perhaps it is $250 for the merchandise.

As one bunco cop explains it, the merchandise is often worth very little, and the prospect is conned into believing that the real "opportunity" is a chance to invest in a distributorship, a franchise which authorizes the prospect to recruit salesmen and receive commissions on their sales. The prospect is pressured to "become a member of the company" immediately, and many sign on the spot and go forth to recruit salesmen.

The salesmen they recruit are then offered the "opportunity" of becoming members of the company and recruit other salesmen who will have that same "opportunity" and, before long, the flaw becomes obvious. If this sort of franchising worked, soon everyone in the world would be a distributor and no one would be left to sell soap or to buy soap.

Since distributorships can cost thousands of dollars, this is no petty graft. Thousands of people all over the United States have lost their life savings to the pyramid franchise bunks. The one thing that distinguishes the swindlers from the legitimate companies such as Avon or Fuller Brush is that the swindlers are not much interested in selling merchandise. They are interested in bringing in "members of the company," who will invest in distributorships.

Pyramid selling has been outlawed in some states. This has not stopped the schemers. Some simply move to another state and lure their victims with offers of transportation and entertainment at posh resort areas such as Las Vegas.

If the day comes when tougher laws on a national level, tighter law enforcement, and bad publicity force the chain-distributorship cons out of business, they will probably go back to the simpler things of life — such as chain letters, which may work for about two weeks at a time, at which point the pyramid will touch ground.

Chapter 7

THE GUESTS WITH TAKING WAYS

A CASTLE is, by definition, a fortified residence. It is fortified so as to be safe from intruders, and most men think of their homes as their castles. They make sure the locks are adequate, and if they worry about intruders at all they think in terms of burglars, vandals and rapists.

HOW SAFE IS THE AVERAGE HOUSEHOLDER FROM THE BUNCO MAN? Jim Perkins felt very safe the day he left his sister's home in Indianapolis. He was bound for his home in Terre Haute and was secure in his car. He was armored by Detroit. But he was tired and he dreaded the long drive alone. So, when he saw a young hitchhiker at the edge of town, he stopped.

The young man was clean-cut, scrubbed, and had a suitcase at his feet. Leaning against the suitcase was a sign with the single word "West" on it.

"I'm going as far as Terre Haute," said Perkins. "That any help to you?"

"Sure is, mister. Thanks."

The suitcase and the sign were tossed into the back seat, and the young man got into the car. "I was beginning to be afraid no one would ever stop," he said.

"I often pick up a hitchhiker here," said Perkins. "Gives me somebody to talk to. All I ask is you don't go to sleep and don't throw your cigarette ashes on the floor."

"I don't smoke," said the passenger.

"Good. Where you headed?"

The young man didn't quite know. He was simply headed West. He'd been laid off at his last job, and there hadn't been another job open for a qualified mechanic. There hadn't been another job open for anyone. He'd even applied for janitorial work and been turned down. He'd run through his unemployment insurance. "I have to do something," he explained to Jim. "I can't just sit and rot. If I get to a town where there's something

56

moving, I'll settle there. You can tell a lot about new towns. If the help wanted sections of the papers are fat, maybe you've got a chance."

Jim Perkins remembered his own youth. His father had held a job all during the depression. Not too many men had been that lucky. Perkins remembered the men on the road, moving, looking for the job that was sure to be open in the next town. He remembered the hungry men who'd come to his mother's door. Not one of them had ever been turned away.

"You had lunch today?" Jim asked the young man.

The young man nodded.

"Where'd you sleep last night?" asked Jim.

"The 'Y'," said the young man.

Jim took his eyes off the road long enough to squint skeptically at his passenger. "The 'Y'?" he demanded. "How much did it cost you?"

The young man looked away, out the window. "It's — it's pretty cheap," he said softly.

"As cheap as the bus station?" asked Jim.

The young man looked back at Jim. "How'd you guess?"

Jim grinned the superior grin of one who has been through one depression, and knows all the angles. "It used to be the hobo jungles and the train depots," he said. "And the parks. I remember the guys in the parks. They'd wrap newspapers around themselves, inside their coats, to keep out the cold."

By the time they reached the outskirts of Terre Haute, it was dusk. "You can let me off anywhere along here," said Perkins' passenger. "Maybe I can pick up another ride before dark."

"And maybe you can't," said Perkins shortly. "Look, why not come home with me and get something to eat? My wife's a great cook."

"I've got some cash," protested the young man.

"So save it. Is a good meal going to hurt you?"

The youthful hitchhiker protested, not too loudly, and he went home with Perkins. As it turned out, the boy had nice manners. He knew how to handle his knife and fork. He stood when Mrs. Perkins came into the room and he stood when she went out and he held her chair for her when she sat down to dinner. He enjoyed the roast chicken. He talked of his home, a farm back in Ohio. "You can't really make it with a small farm now," he said. "After my dad died, we sold out. My mother's living with my sister and her husband. She's not too happy there, I'm afraid. Isn't there something about no house being big enough for two women? Anyway, when I get located maybe I can send for her and she can keep house for me."

Mrs. Perkins' heart melted, and immediately after dinner she marched Mr. Perkins to the kitchen, where they could talk without being overheard by their young guest.

The upshot was that Perkins insisted that the young hitchhiker spend the night in the spare bedroom.

It was sheer chance that Jim Perkins awoke in the middle of the night and decided that he was thirsty. He got up and headed for the bathroom to get a drink of water. When he passed the door of the spare bedroom he paused and listened. Not a sound. Perkins got his water and went back into his bedroom, and as he passed the dresser he happened to touch it. There wasn't anything there. He'd put his watch on the dresser when he'd gotten ready for bed, and his car keys and his wallet and a little pile of change. Now the things were gone.

In the next three minutes, Perkins discovered that the nice, openfaced young hitchhiker was gone, and so was the sterling flatware and Mrs. Perkins' engagement ring, which she'd left on the windowsill above the sink when she'd done the dishes. The garage was empty, too. Having a set of car keys at his disposal, what could be more natural than that the young hitchhiker would use them to make off with the car?

Mr. Perkins called the police. Fifteen minutes later a clean-cut young man was picked up a mile from the Perkins house. He was in the act of changing the license plates on the Perkins' car. That neat suitcase held a collection of stolen license plates plus, of course, Mrs. Perkins' engagement ring and her sterling.

Mr. Perkins was lucky — much luckier than other kindly drivers who have picked up hitchhikers. And he learned a lesson: Con men are convincing. It's their business to be convincing, and the thieving hitchhiker only wanted to get into somebody's home.

The man who offers a lift to a girl may become the victim of another nasty little racket. The girl may threaten to tear her own clothes, scream, jump out of the car, accuse the driver of assaulting her or attempting to assault her. The payoff on this trick may be ten dollars, or twenty, or whatever the victim has in his pockets. Many men are glad to get off that easily and some never complain to the police. Even if no one wearing a badge believes the girl, what will the neighbors say? Word can get around.

The thieving hitchhiker isn't the only con artist who will attempt to invade a victim's home. The ploys are varied and new ones keep cropping up.

THERE ARE EXTREMELY CHARMING CON MEN WHO ARE LOOKING FOR BUSINESS PARTNERS. Harry K. Miles, a fifty-two-year-old plumbing contractor, was approached at his place of business by a man who represented himself as a dealer in fine china, porcelain, and antique gems. The man was in his early sixties, of average height, white-haired, and with a pallid complexion. He began to discuss proposed renovations required in his shop. Miles reported that he was extremely articulate, and that very soon the conversation drifted to the man's purported specialties and the man told several stories of famous jewels. He confessed to ill health and implied that he was trying to find a partner who would help him run his business. He also complained of loneliness and told Miles that he lived at a nearby apartment hotel. It was late in the aftertnoon, and Miles invited the man to have dinner in his home.

At dinner, the gentlemanly guest continued his discussion of fine jewelry and porcelain. He admired Mrs. Miles' engagement ring. He expressed dismay when told that the ring was not insured, and consented to examine several pieces of jewelry which had been left to Mrs. Miles by an aunt. He informed Mrs. Miles that a brooch which she believed was set with garnets was, in fact, set with rubies, and at the end of the evening he agreed to take the jewelry to an appraiser who was reliable. He gave Mrs. Miles a receipt which he wrote on the back of his business card and he left the Miles residence in a taxi.

Three days later, Miles became uneasy and attempted to contact the "jeweler" by telephone. The telephone number on the business card proved to be the telephone number of a bar and grill.

The address on the card was the address of a hardware store. The suspect was unknown at the apartment hotel where he claimed to live. Miles was unable to identify the suspect from mug books.

The dinner guest who claimed to need a partner didn't really need any help at all. He did his thing very well. He got away with a diamond engagement ring, an antique brooch set with garnets, a pair of gold earrings, and a pearl necklace. None of the pieces was insured.

THE FAKE "INSPECTOR" IS ANOTHER MENACE TO THE HOUSEHOLDER. At approximately 2:00 one afternoon, Mrs. Jonathan Herbert, a housewife who lives in Columbus, Ohio, answered her doorbell. Two men in blue coveralls stood on her doormat and told her they were trying to run down a gas leak which was somewhere in the neighborhood. They asked where the gas line entered the house. She showed them, and watched from the porch as they examined the place. Suddenly she saw a spurt of flame, and one of the men came running to her and asked for a wet rag to put out the fire.

Mrs. Herbert ran into her kitchen, grabbed a dish towel, wet it, and ran back to the front door. The fire seemed to be out, but the men asked if they could come in to use the telephone. Mrs. Herbert gladly agreed.

One of the men dialed a number on the telephone, then said, "It's okay. We found it, and you can take that pressure off." He listened briefly, then said, "Okay, we'll tell the customer," and he hung up.

He then informed Mrs. Herbert that she would have to vacate the house for two or three days while they repaired the dama,je to the gas line.

Mrs. Herbert was distressed and, like most citizens, very much afraid of escaping gas. She did delay, however, and told the men that she would have to call her husband.

"Okay," said the man who seemed to be spokesman for the pair. "We'll finish our inspection while you make the call."

While Mrs. Herbert telephoned, the men went into the kitchen and then out into the back yard. Mr. Herbert promised to come home immediately and Mrs. Herbert hung up and went in search of the "inspectors."

The two men were gone. Mrs. Herbert discovered almost immediately that the wallet had been taken from her purse, which was on the kitchen counter, and that an undetermined amount of cash which she kept as an emergency fund was gone from a teapot which had been on top fo the refrigerator. When Mr. Herbert arrived home, he called the gas company and could learn of no leak in the neighborhood.

Mrs. Herbert was able to identify the two suspects from police photographs, and warrants were issues for their arrest. As of this writing, the two suspects have not been apprehended.

FEW WOMEN CAN RESIST THE "BABY BURGLAR." One victim, Mrs. Thomas Greene, reported that two women rang her doorbell one morning and asked for a small donation for a youth center. Mrs. Greene put a quarter into the slot of a container which the older woman held out for her. The second woman, who was approximately twenty-four-years-old, was carrying a baby. Mrs. Greene estimated the age of the child as about six months, and reported that the baby began to whimper. The younger woman asked if she could have a drink of water for the baby. Mrs. Greene took the young woman and the baby to the kitchen and gave the young woman a glass of water. After the baby took a few sips, the young woman returned the water to Mrs. Greene, thanked her, and returned to the older woman, who had waited in the living room. The two suspects then left the Green home with the baby.

At 2:00 that afternoon Mrs. Greene discovered that her change purse was missing from her handbag and that her wallet had been emptied of cash and the bills replaced with pieces of newspaper.

Police, commenting on the Greene case, stated that Mrs. Greene was the victim of a tried-and-true bunco scheme called the "baby burglary." The baby burglars needn't be artistic or even particularly clever. All they need is one baby and an excuse to ring the victim's doorbell and persuade her to get out her pocketbook. Hardly a woman on earth could refuse a drink of water to a thirsty child. When the woman with the baby trails the housewife through the house to the kitchen, the second woman goes through the housewife's purse.

THE CON ARTIST WHO DOES NOT HAVE ACCESS TO A BABY MAY TRY RELIGION. In Miami a fifty-three-year-old woman named

Hilda Jackson earned her living as a chambermaid in a hotel. One Sunday morning she was called upon by a woman who said she was a messenger of the Church of the New Awakening. The woman spoke to Mrs. Jackson of the Second Coming and they prayed together. Afterward they talked about Mrs. Jackson's work, and Mrs. Jackson took the woman into her bedroom to show her a new dress she was making. A purse was hanging on the knob of the bedroom door. The woman left shortly after. The next morning Mrs. Jackson discovered that thirty dollars which had been in her purse was missing. In its place was a roll of newspaper.

The theft was reported to the police and a description of the suspect was given. To date, no arrest has been made.

If Religion Doesn't Work, There Is Always the "Termite" Dodge. Harold Evans, a forty-three-year-old insurance salesman, was approached in his home by a man who offered to inspect the house for termites. The man looked at the areas under the front and back steps, then came into the house and rapped on the walls. He asked Evans to step into the kitchen and rap on the walls there while he listened. Evans did so. When Evans returned to the dining room, where he had left the "termite inspector," the man had disappeared. Evans reported that the silver flatware and several small golf trophies were missing.

The suspect was apprehended three days later in another town. He had been caught in the act of searching sideboard drawers when his intended victim's wife returned unexpectedly from the supermarket. He fled from the house but was picked up by police three blocks away.

Even the Pensioners, the Elderly Who Have to Watch Every Penny Must Guard Against the Intrusive Con Artist. Sometimes He Masquerades as a Social Worker. Hilda Griswold, a widow in her seventies, lived alone in a little bungalow in Denver and took good care that her tiny income would stretch from the first of one month to the first of the next.

One morning Mrs. Griswold was called upon by a fiftyish man who carried a clipboard to which were attached many forms and papers.

"I'm from the Denver County Department of Human Resources," he said. "My name is Samuel Moore. May I come in?"

He was neat and clean and looked respectable. She let him in.

He seated himself on one side of the living room sofa, his knees together and his clipboard on his lap. He removed a ball-point pen from his shirt pocket and held it ready.

"What did you say your name was?" she asked.

"Moore. Sam Moore. Fron the County Department of Human Resources."

"I don't believe I've heard of that organization."

Moore laughed. "Frankly, it used to be called the Welfare Department. But somebody decided the new name sounded better."

"But I'm not on welfare."

"Oh no. We know that. And we intend to see that you're not. That's why I'm here."

"I don't understand."

"Let me explain, Mrs. Griswold. You see, we know who's receiving welfare payments and who isn't. We also know who might be entitled to them. And we like to talk to those people about their spending habits — saving habits, really — to make sure they stay *off* the county welfare roles."

Moore then proceeded to ask Mrs. Griswold a great many questions and to fill out blanks on the forms on his clipboard. He asked about her late husband, her children, her doctor, the names of friends who might be called in an emergency. He asked about her house, her bank accounts, unemployment insurance, disability insurance, veterans benefits, social security, and how much she spent monthly at Sears.

And, bewildered and a little afraid of all this "official" attention, Mrs. Griswold answered his questions. She even confided to him that she kept a small amount of cash in the house for emergencies — a few hundred, in case of a crisis. He seemed concerned that she might not be able to handle a crisis. He seemed relieved that she had such foresight, that she kept the cash well hidden in the toe of a slipper.

He then asked to use the bathroom, and after doing so, he departed.

Mrs. Griswold soon discovered that her slippers were where they belonged, in the bedroom next to the bathroom, but that her emergency fund was gone.

The county had no record of Samuel Moore and had not, of course, instigated any survey such as he had conducted.

SOMETIMES THE GUESTS WITH THE TAKING WAYS CAN BE APPREHENDED. IT IS FAR BETTER IF THE HOUSEHOLDER CAN BE EDUCATED TO PROTECT HIMSELF, TO KEEP THE THIEVES OUT. Again, good relations between the community and the police are vital. The public should be warned not to permit strangers to enter a house or an apartment for any reason whatsoever.

The woman with the thirsty baby can be kept waiting on the doorstep for that glass of water. The housewife may feel rude, but she will be safer, and when she carries the water from the kitchen to the front door (which she has locked while she went to the kitchen) it will be just as wet as if the "mother" had trailed her to the sink.

Inspectors who say they are from the gas company (or the electric company, or whatever) should never be admitted to a home until the householder has called the company to verify that there is a problem.

Hitchhikers can be a menace. Law enforcement officers should do all they can to discourage hitchhiking. In some areas it is illegal, and where such laws exist they should be enforced.

Encourage the use of chain locks and peep holes in doors.

And above all, when a victim has been foolish enough to admit a con man to his house, don't embarrass him. Take the report, get all the details possible and send out the description. You might get lucky and save the next householder who leaves his drawbridge down.

Chapter 8

EVERYONE NEEDS A ROOF
OVER HIS HEAD

THE real estate business is tricky. One real estate salesman, in a moment of semi-alcoholic honesty, confided to one of the authors that, "We're all crooks." He did not actually mean that he broke the law. He only meant that he advised homeowners who wanted to sell their houses to "green up" the lawns with high-powered fertilizers so that they'd look better and not to mention the fact that the roof hadn't been fixed for ten years and that the guarantee on the water heater was about to expire.

The real estate man who also has that quirk of character that makes the confidence man can do dreadful damage to the hopeful house-hunter. He knows the law, which the average person doesn't, and he knows the financial system and how it works, which the average person doesn't.

AMONG THESE SHARPIES ARE THE BROKERS WHO PERSUADE THE GULLIBLE HOMEOWNER TO PUT HIS MONEY DOWN ON A HOUSE WITHOUT FIRST INSISTING ON A PROPER TITLE SEARCH. The ghastly experience of Walter Boyd is typical.

Boyd was an average young American, neither poor nor rich. He has been married for three years, had one child and a second on the way. He and his wife lived in an apartment which was too small, inconvenient, and in an inner-city neighborhood where the schools were bad and the traffic was so heavy that pushing a baby carriage to the supermarket was an exercise in courage.

Boyd had no savings to speak of, and he needed a house — not a cluttered apartment, but a house.

When his father-in-law offered to lend Boyd the money for a down payment on a home, Boyd accepted the offer. He didn't want to go into hock to the old man, but he knew that when the new baby arrived the small, inconvenient apartment would be impossible.

Boyd and his wife began their house-hunting on a Sunday, and they first toured the tract homes in the newer suburbs. The homes were beautiful, and they had all the latest gadgets and wall-to-wall carpeting. They were also far, far too expensive.

The Boyds retreated to the older suburbs where the homes were smaller and the lawns weren't so well kept up. In a tacky little real estate office which was tucked into a store front between a shoe repair shop and a drug store, they encountered a sympathetic individual named Faulkner — Jimmie Faulkner. He seemed to understand their problems perfectly, including the problem of financing.

He was most encouraging, however, and Walter Boyd began to take heart.

"I think we've got something you can handle," said Faulkner. "You don't want to bankrupt yourself for a house, you know. You've got your whole future ahead of you."

Faulkner took a set of keys from a pegboard on the wall. "We have one place that will take a little fixing up, but it's basically in good shape. We had to foreclose on it last month."

"You were carrying the mortgage yourself?" said Boyd. This didn't seem usual to him.

"Arkham Realty does that a lot," explained Faulkner. "Mr. Morris, our president, has the capital to invest and he believes in real estate. You can't lose on it, and it's about the only thing you can't lose on. We can give you better interest rates than the bank, and at the same time Arkham makes a bit. Come on. I'll show you the house. My car's right outside."

Jimmie Faulkner's car was air conditioned, which was pleasant indeed, and Faulkner drove the Boyds to a one-story house on a pleasant, shady street.

"School's around the corner and two blocks down," he said as he held the door for Mrs. Boyd. "Your children can walk there when they get old enough."

That was a good thing to say to Mrs. Boyd.

"The foundation planting needs pruning," Faulkner apologized as he led the Boyds up the front walk. "We've kept the lawn trimmed. Nothing makes a place look seedier than an overgrown lawn."

The front door of the house opened with a slight, sticky lurch and they were in the living room. The carpeting was wall-to-wall, although not spotlessly new. Mrs. Boyd could see the place where someone had once had a big sofa. They went on through to a kitchen which had no gadgets, but which was big enough, and with plenty of cupboards.

There was no stove, but Jimmie Faulkner assured them that they could pick up a second-hand stove for a song. Watch the ads in the classified section. With all the built-ins in the newer places, people were dying to get rid of stoves and refrigerators. They'd almost pay you to take one away. And Boyd could hire a small trailer and move it himself.

Beyond the kitchen was a service porch with plenty of room for a washer, and beyond that was the back yard, with a few neglected rose bushes and a nice elm tree.

There was only one bath, but there was one fair-sized bedroom and two smaller ones. The house would do. It wasn't the automated, air-conditioned, decorator-designed American dream, but it would do. It was a beginning and the neighborhood looked okay. Best of all, the price was right. The down payment would not be too much of a blow, and Boyd could handle the monthly carrying charges. In fact, these would be less than the rent on that crowded, untidy apartment.

In no time, the Boyds were back in the real estate office; Jimmie Faulkner was filling out a long, complicated form and, in the kindliest manner possible, was asking how long Boyd had been at his present job. What did he earn a year? Education? Finished college, eh? Good! Hard to get far these days without a college education. And did Walter have any other debts? And how about insurance? Jimmie Faulkner approved of insurance. Every young married man ought to have it.

When the form was completed, Jimmie Faulkner said, "This will have to be approved by our president, of course. He's never in on Sundays, but I think he'll go along. And we'll check your credit. You'll hear from us in a day or two."

Boyd put down a hundred-dollar deposit to hold the house.

"This will be returned," said Faulkner, "if the deal doesn't go through. I'll talk to Mr. Morris first thing in the morning, and we'll get right to work on your application."

The Boyds went back to their apartment and waited. Faulkner called on Wednesday. Their application had been approved. There would be papers to sign and the down payment to pay the Arkham Company, but there wasn't any reason they couldn't move into their house the first of next month.

Mrs. Boyd's father was driven to the new house; he made a quick tour of inspection and announced that at least it was better than that two-by-four apartment. He had $1,500 deposited to Boyd's checking account to take care of the down payment. And, because he prided himself on his business acumen, he made Boyd sign a promissory note.

The Boyds combed the classified ads. Jimmie Faulkner had been right. They got a nearly new refrigerator and a stove for almost nothing. Boyd hauled the things out to the house in a trailer, with an assist from one of his office buddies, and he and his wife moved into the house.

Boyd painted and puttered. His wife cleaned and lined cupboard shelves with paper. And every month Boyd made his payment to the Arkham Realty Company.

Three months after they moved, a bewildering thing happened. Mr. and Mrs. Boyd were informed that they were about to be evicted.

Boyd did not own that house. The Arkham Realty Company did not own it, and indeed never had owned that house. The house was the property of a man Boyd had never heard of — a James Conners. Conners had acquired an FHA-guaranteed loan to purchase the house several months before. He had never paid a dime on that loan. Quite understandably, the bank which held the mortgage wanted the money.

Mrs. Boyd thought they should take the problem to her father. Boyd recoiled at the very idea, and he luckily did not take the problem to Jimmie Faulkner. He took it to a friend who was a lawyer.

The lawyer knew exactly where to take the problem — and did so quickly. Since the FHA was involved, he took it to the Federal Bureau of Investigation. Jimmie Faulkner, who was the entire Arkham Realty Company, had an uncomfortable interview with a man from the FBI. The interview occurred just as Faulkner was packing his briefcase, preparing to abandon his office without even bothering to sell his second-hand desk.

Faulkner did not leave town, as he had planned. He stayed to face charges of fraud brought by the United States Attorney's Office for further investigation of Faulkner, and his business revealed that Faulkner had been busy in the area for at least six months.

Faulkner was a bunco man with a scheme that was bound to work — for a while. Faulkner would find a house that needed a new owner. He would then locate some person who was eligible for FHA financing and offer to pay $100 to $500 for the use of this financing. Faulkner had charm, and he was a first-rate salesman. He was able to convince his unwitting accomplices that they were making $100 or so just for signing a few papers, and that their obligation would begin and end there.

With the aid of his ghost owners, Faulkner was able to acquire a portfolio of real estate for relatively little money. The house which Walter Boyd bought, or thought he bought, was valued at $15,000. For a very small percentage of this amount, Faulkner was able to get the house. The title, of course, was in the name of the ghost owner. Faulkner had a number of ghost owners, and he had pocketed numbers of down payments and monthly payments and had calculated almost to the day how long it would take for the lending institutions to realize that payments on the houses he had sold were in arrears. Luckily for Walter Boyd, Faulkner waited too long before making his exit.

Some of the money which Boyd had put into the house went down the drain, but Boyd was able to regain part of his down payment, do some refinancing, and start over. He and his wife managed to remain in the house which he had "bought" from the understanding Jimmie Faulkner, but this time he made sure he had clear title to the house. This time he had a lawyer, and there was a title search.

According to one law enforcement officer who was interviewed, the most maddening thing about bunco men who operate in the real estate field is that the victim often doesn't complain. "He's just a little guy who's used to being caught in the system, and he figures he somehow someway did something dumb and got caught in the system again. He can lose his life savings and maybe he's bitter, but it doesn't occur to him to go to a lawyer or call a cop.

"Even if he does call a cop, and the law moves in on the bunco artist, the con usually gets off with a suspended sentence. Hell, if a kid steals a car and goes for a joy ride, he can wind up spending two years in the pen, but these worms who take an honest guy for his last dime get suspended sentences. It's enough to make you throw up."

If you are lucky enough to get a complaint on this kind of bunk, move fast. Move before the crooked salesman can leave town, or before he can transfer his funds to some dummy corporation or a bank account in a fictitious name and declare bankruptcy.

And if you want to throw up, do it later.

THE USE OF GHOST OWNERS IS ONLY ONE WAY A CROOKED REAL ESTATE MAN CAN TAKE THE UNWARY HOUSE-HUNTER. THERE IS ALSO THE "SALE" OF CONDEMNED HOMES. In any state where freeways, throughways or expressways are under construction, homes must be condemned and acquired by the state to make way for the new roads. These houses are offered for sale to buyers who are willing to move them to new locations. Buyers have been taken in by bunco artists who offer these vacant freeway houses for sale. If the purchaser is incautious enough to acquire a freeway home without assuring himself that the "seller" has the right to sell, he may put down a deposit and not realize he has been conned until his house mover shows up at the freeway site. The house mover will then encounter resistance from legitimate state employees at the site. By this time, the bunco man may be in Nome, Alaska, peddling igloos to restless Eskimos.

THE PROSPECTIVE BUYER IS NOT THE ONLY TARGET OF THE REAL ESTATE BUNK. EVEN THE RENTER MUST BE ALERT. In one type of rental bunk, the con artist first rents a house. He doesn't use his own name, since con artists are adverse to using their own names. (Some of them have used so many names that they have forgotten what was written on their birth certificates in the beginning.)

Under the alias he has chosen, the con man establishes credit (and this can be done very easily, as shown in Chapter 10); has his gas, electricity, and telephone connected in his new residence; and visits the local furniture emporium to order beds, bureaus, living room chairs, a TV or two, and the appliances he will need to keep himself in comfort.

He then places an advertisement in the papers offering his house for rent. Prospective tenants show up and either are enchanted with the house or badly need a place to live. The con man produces a lease, or perhaps announces that he doesn't believe in leases. Either way, he demands the first and last month's rent in advance, plus a despoit for cleaning. The prospective tenant pays, and the moving date is set for several weeks in the future. When the new tenant arrives with his van full of furniture, he finds that the house has already been rented to seventeen people, all of whom expected to take up occupancy on the same date.

The con man, naturally, has decamped several days before moving day, taking with him his new furniture and appliances — none of which are paid for. He can sell the furniture at a discount and disappear to another town, to begin all over again. The telephone company, the gas company, and the electric company will whistle for their money.

In this type of bunk, the con artist is renting a house which he does not own. It is also possible for a prospective tenant to encounter a con man who is renting a house which he *does* own, at least at the moment. The "rent skimmer" is the bunco man who keeps himself informed on foreclosures. When some poor soul is about to lose his home because he's had financial reverses, he may be contacted by a rent skimmer who offers to purchase the home — quickly and at a very low price. Sometimes he offers the down-and-out homeowner as little as a hundred dollars in exchange for a deed. The owner figures he has nothing to lose, since he is going to be dispossessed anyway. He forgets, for the moment, that there is a waiting period between publication of a notice to foreclose and the actual foreclosure date. The original owner thus loses up to three months' free occupancy of the house, which he is selling for almost nothing.

The rent skimmer immediately rents the house, collects the first and last months' rent, plus the cleaning fee, then returns at the beginning of the second month and perhaps at the beginning of the third month to collect the rent "due" him. At the end of the third month, the new tenant, who has just arranged the living room furniture to his wife's satisfaction, has to move because the house is repossessed. The renter is out one month's rent.

The con artists who specialize in swindling would-be renters are not able to take as big a bite out of the average citizen's bank account as those who "sell" homes, but they can certainly frustrate the bunco cop. The person who seeks only to be a tenant has almost no defense against these thieves. It isn't customary to engage a lawyer before signing a lease. It isn't customary for a renter to ask the purported owner of a property who holds the mortgage on that property.

The only defense against rent skimmers and their ilk is a good public information program. If one is operating in your jurisdiction, publicize the operation. Put the prospective tenants on guard. Encourage them to investigate before they pay the first and last month's rent and the cleaning fee. Encourage them to go to the house next door or across the street or down the block and ring the bell. They can always tell whoever answers that bell that they're "thinking of moving into the house at 236" and they can ask about the neighborhood and about the house.

If they learn that the present tenant just moved into the house, they may suspect that they are dealing with a con artist who is renting an already rented house and who will depart with their funds — and they may call the bunco squad.

Probably they won't, but you can always hope.

Chapter 9

EXPLOITING THE
AMERICAN WILDERNESS

IN the 1920s the con artists discovered Florida. It had been previously discovered by Ponce de Leon, who was really looking for the fountain of youth. What he found was not eternal youth, but a land with a pleasant climate and many, many swamps. The con men who invaded Florida some four hundred years later took careful note of the climate and acquired title to a number of swamps, plus some tidelands which were under water twelve hours out of every day. They then peddled this land to people from harsher climates — to chilly New Englanders and weary businessmen from Illinois and Indiana. The great Florida land swindle came to a crashing halt when the new owners of these damp lots arrived to view their property and discovered that they would have to wade, swim or own a submarine in order to enjoy their investment.

One would think that the publicity following the Florida scandal would have put an end to criminal exploitation of undeveloped land, but it hasn't. For one thing, America has not run out of wilderness, and America is not about to run out of wilderness. For another, many people hold fast to the belief that land is the only truly safe investment.

The bunco men take advantage of this in a number of ways. "INVEST IN THE PLANNED COMMUNITY OF THE FUTURE," INVITE THE CON MEN. "LOTS ARE STILL AVAILABLE, BUT THEY'RE GOING FAST." Mr. and Mrs. Ellery Cushman got caught by this bait when they were on their way home from a rock-hunting trip in Nevada. They were enticed off the highway by a sign indicating that Paradise Mesa, a new community, was being created in the desert, forty miles from the nearest town. Paradise Mesa would offer its residents their own shopping center, including supermarket, pharmacy, specialty shops, gas stations, restaurants, a country club, two golf courses, and three community swimming pools.

The Cushmans, in their early sixties, were thinking of retiring and leaving smog-bound Los Angeles. Paradise Mesa, when the Cushmans first saw it, consisted of a network of paved streets, two houses, and a trailer. The sales office was in the trailer, and a young salesman eagerly displayed the plan for the new town.

There was plenty of water, he said, since seven artesian wells had been dug. Homesites which had already been sold were colored blue on the town map, and the place where the golf courses would be laid out were a pleasant green. There were architects' sketches of the proposed shopping center and the country club. If the Cushmans wished, the development company would build a home for them on the plot they selected, and the salesman offered several floor plans. Even if the Cushmans didn't want to build right away, the salesman urged them to acquire their lot, since the land was going fast. The salesman took them on a tour of the place so they could select the lot most pleasing to them, although one piece of Nevada desert looks much like another. "Even if you never move here, you can hardly lose," he pointed out. "The down payment on the land is only $750, and the monthly payments will run you under fifty dollars. As Paradise Mesa grows, your land has got to appreciate. Five years from now you can sell it for twice what you paid."

Five years later, Mr. and Mrs. Ellery Cushman were on their way home from a rock-hunting trip. Mr. Cushman had long since written off the $750 he had put down for his piece of land in Paradise Mesa and the monthly payments he had made for almost two years. When he saw the familiar, but now weathered and weary, sign on the side road, he turned off and he and Mrs. Cushman again toured that desert Eden.

Paradise Mesa consisted of two houses, now beginning to bake to pieces in the fierce sunlight, a network of paved streets, and two parched areas where the golf courses had been planned. The trailer which had been the sales office was gone. Who needed it? Every lot had been sold "as an investment which is bound to appreciate." And, since all the purchasers had sat in San Francisco or San Diego or Los Angeles and waited for their retirement to come due, and for their desert land to appreciate, Paradise Mesa had never become a community.

The Cushmans could not accuse the developers of Paradise Mesa of deliberate intent to defraud. The seven artesian wells *had* been dug and the streets had been laid out. If only two hardy couples had built homes in Paradise Mesa, one could not blame the developers for failing to go ahead with their plans for the shopping center, the country club, and the golf courses. The contract which Mr. Cushman had signed did not actually guarantee the shopping center and the other goodies. The Cushmans, and many others who had put money into Paradise Mesa, were the victims of their own bad judgment. They had bought too quickly and under pressure.

Sometimes it is possible to bring charges against the fast-talking operators who exploit the citizen's hunger for a piece of American soil if the law enforcement officer can get enough complaints to show the pattern which indicates intent to defraud, and if he can move quickly enough to nail the "developers" before they transfer their funds to some finance company (which they may actually have formed for this purpose, but which supposedly has no connection with the original development company).

In one California case, charges were brought against a "developer" who had sold the same prime lot in a "planned community of the future" to at least fifty people. It was a lot on the top of a hill, the only one in the entire development with a view of the valley below. When the purchasers of this lovely lot signed on the dotted line, and later returned to inspect their new property, they learned that what they had actually bought was inferior property, down on the flatlands, away from the view, the breeze, and anything else that might make their bit of the future community attractive.

In another case, a number of residents of San Francisco answered an alluring advertisement that offered a free plane ride to Las Vegas, free overnight accommodations at a motel, and ten dollars with which to gamble at any of the local casinos. It was a come-on sponsored by a group of sharpies who had acquired dubious title to a patch of desert outside the city of Vegas — quite far outside. The plane ride happened on schedule and the guest of the developers were allowed to check into a motel. They were then taken for a ride out into the desert and were given a sales pitch. They were invited to put their money into another wonderful "community of the future."

One of the guests had more sales resistance than some others. He flatly refused even to consider purchasing a hunk of heat-seared desolation. The salesman who had been suave and persuasive lost his cool completely. He got into his air-conditioned car and drove off, leaving the man stranded and steaming. The San Franciscan was both frightened and furious, but he managed to make his way to a road and got a ride back to town, and the "developers" were nailed immediately for coercion.

It very quickly became apparent that there was not going to be any planned community. There was not going to be anything. The corporation which had been set up to market the land hadn't tried very hard to assure themselves that their right to do so was indisputable. Even if they had tried, their chances of ever really clearing titles to the various parcels of property would have been slim. Much of the American wilderness has been prospected and claims have been staked. Homesteaders have tried to live on the land, then have abandoned it and failed to keep up the taxes. Or they have established title to the land, then married and had the land become community property. Heirs have appeared or have not appeared. County courthouses have burned down. Records have been destroyed. It is often anybody's guess who really owns those wide-open spaces.

THE BEST DEFENSE AGAINST THE FLY-BY-NIGHT "DEVELOPER" IS A GOOD PUBLIC INFORMATION PROGRAM. Laws vary from state to state and from county to county, but in almost every area the powers that be want orderly development. It is the only kind that pays off for the area and for the citizen who purchases land in the area.

In most localities, a developer must meet certain requirements before he can legally begin to subdivide vacant land and sell lots. He must usually file plans with the county showing how the lots will be laid out; where the water is coming from; what arrangements have been made for sanitation, flood control, drainage — all the amenities that we take for granted. The prospective purchaser has a right to see these plans. The prospective purchaser should be made aware of this right.

The legitimate developer or subdivider can spend thousands, even millions, readying a tract of wilderness for the market. If he has, the plans and reports will be on file.

There are ways that bootleg land operators can get around these requirements, again depending on the local laws. They may form dummy corporations, for example. There may be a bewildering number of these dummy corporations. The land originally purchased by Company A may be sold in part to Company B, in part to Company C, in part to Company D. The land held by Company C may be divided into two or three or four smaller portions and sold to Companies X, Y and Z. By the time the con men are ready to go into business and start selling building lots to the public, each lot may be about an acre in size and there are heaps and piles and files of papers in the county offices covering the transfers of titles; and it would appear on the surface that no one is subdividing. A large number of owners are putting their lots on the market.

Of course someone is subdividing. The con men who own Company A and who acquired the land in the first place are subdividing. However, they have probably not met the county and state requirements, and they probably do not have the proper maps and plans on file with the county real estate agencies and the state board which controls development, and a public report on the subdivision or development will probably not be available should an informed member of the public request one.

At which point the law can step in and start ferreting out the truth.

SOME OF THE BUNCO MEN WHO DEAL IN WILDERNESS PROPERTIES DON'T EVEN PRETEND TO BE DEVELOPERS OR SUBDIVIDERS. SOME JUST INVITE THE CITY-WORN CITIZEN TO "ACQUIRE YOUR OWN MOUNTAIN RETREAT" OR "GET AWAY FROM IT ALL IN THE COOL, GREEN NORTHWEST." They may have acquired a perfectly legitimate title to some stretch of forest or some mountain slope. They may appear at county fairs, home shows, and the like with maps of the idyllic region they are marketing, with photographs of pine forests and sparkling streams. They may transport their prospective customers to these remote havens, where there is no smog, no noise (except for the twittering of birds), and where the landowner can, if he wishes, put up his own mountain cabin and get away from it all. The air is clean and the wind is cool and the streams are alive with trout.

It is pleasant indeed. The sucker, tired of his city apartment and the daily hassels with traffic and the long lines at the check-out counters of supermarkets, may sign for his hunk of wilderness then and there.

Quite often, after he *has* signed, he discovers that that trout-filled stream rises four feet every spring, completely flooding his land, and that there is a very good reason why there are no traffic noises — since there are no roads. Also, no markets, no electricity and, except for the stream, no water supply.

AGAIN, UNLESS THE PUBLIC IS PUT ON ITS GUARD AGAINST THE CON MEN WHO DEAL IN LAND, THERE MAY NOT BE MUCH THE LAW CAN DO. THE CONS WILL HAVE COLLECTED THEIR LOOT AND FADED AWAY. PUBLICITY IS THE ONLY ANSWER TO THE THIEVING SALESMAN WHO DEALS IN THE UNSPOILED PORTIONS OF THE AMERICAN WILDERNESS. The truth is that many unspoiled portions of America remain unspoiled because they simply are not habitable. At one time, one of the authors encountered an extremely charming gentleman who made a living of sorts selling lots on the Kona Coast of Hawaii to residents of Los Angeles. The encounter with the land salesman was not completely pleasant, since he bashed into the author's car. However, he assured the author that his insurance company would take care of the damage; courtesies and license plate numbers were exchanged; and, after getting an estimate from a couple of body shops, the author attempted to collect damages. The author discovered that:

1. the salesman was driving a car which was not registered in his name;
2. the plates on the car had belonged to the previous owner of the car, who had notified the Bureau of Motor Vehicles several months prior to the incident that he had sold the car;
3. so far as anyone could ascertain, the salesman did not have auto insurance;
4. the salesman did not even have a local habitation, since his "company" operated out of a post office box.

Possibly the Hawaiian land which the man was peddling to Angelenos was good land. However, when one considers the breathtaking ease with which the man told lies, one suspects that that land on the Kona Coast might be covered with lava. One suspects that it might be in an area where even more lava could come trickling out of the volcanic fissures in the hillsides at any moment.

We are about where we were in the 1920s when the suede shoe men sold those swamps in Florida. Today it is the great American desert or the cool green northwest or Hawaii, but it doesn't matter. If no one can live on it, if the land is no good, and if people are not warned, they may continue to purchase land without investigating, and sometimes without even seeing the land.

Chapter 10

A GOOD CREDIT RATING
IS NOT NECESSARILY GOOD

PEOPLE who have money to invest in building, but not quite enough money, are marks for the bunco men who operate the "advanced fee" swindle. Doctors are pushovers for this bunk, and, as one expert put it, they can't yell too loudly because they don't want to lose the confidence of their patients. Also, doctors frequently do have surplus capital and many are looking for tax shelters.

The case of a group of doctors in Michigan is typical. There were seven of them — an internist, an obstetrician, a dermatologist, a pediatrician, a surgeon, a roentgenologist and a psychiatrist. All were good friends who had referred patients to one another for years. They got together and decided to form a medical group and build their own building.

All of the doctors had surplus money to invest in the new building. However, they discovered when they discussed their plan with a firm of architects that they needed additional financing. The medical men approached several banks, but the loan officers at the banks were reluctant to underwrite the project to the required extent.

The doctors were stymied until one of them was approached at his country club by a person who introduced himself as J. P. Alleman. Alleman was at the club as the guest of another member.

"You're Doctor Smith, aren't you?" said the man named Alleman.

Doctor Smith, the internist, was sipping at the first of the two martinis he allowed himself each day, and he only grunted and scowled and thought to himself that he was encountering another of those pushy people who try to get free medical advice at bars and cocktail parties.

"Can I buy you a drink?" asked Alleman.

"No thanks. I'm set," said Dr. Smith.

Alleman ordered a drink for himself and ignored the fact that the doctor was trying to put him down. "Harry Halstead was telling me that you're planning to put up a medical building on that lot at Poplar and Evans," said Alleman.

Dr. Smith admitted that he and his friends had an option on the property.

"I might be interested," said Alleman.

Dr. Smith put his drink down. "Interested?"

"In a piece of the project," said Alleman. "Halstead said the bankers were giving you a hard time."

The doctor shook his head. "They don't think the idea will pan out," he told the stranger. "They don't think the neighborhood's right for a building like that."

"There isn't a really good medical center in the area," said Alleman. "I checked. I checked you out, too. I think it will work."

Dr. Smith waited. He had found, in his practice, that one learned a great deal about a patient — or anybody else for that matter — not by questioning but simply by taking time and waiting.

"I'm president of the J.P.A. Corporation," said Alleman. "We're interested in investments, developments. If you want to talk to your colleagues, maybe we can get together. Give me a buzz and we can set up a time."

With that, Alleman handed Dr. Smith a business card and drifted off, carrying his drink with him.

Dr. Smith did not wait to have dinner at the country club. He hurried home and called the pediatrician, the dermatology, the obstetrician, the surgeon, the psychiatrist and the roentgenologist. The seven doctors met the next day for lunch and decided that there would be no harm in investigating further the almost casual offer that Alleman had made in the country club the night before.

That afternoon, Dr. Smith called Alleman, and he and Alleman agreed that the medicos would meet in Alleman's office the following Wednesday.

When the doctors arrived at the office of the J.P.A. Corporation, they found that the entire organization consisted of Alleman plus one secretary. The furniture was impressive and the address was prestigious and Alleman was obviously a wheeler-dealer — a money man, pure and simple. He indicated to the group that if further investigation showed their plans to be sound, he might, for a fee, be able to arrange financing with one of the banks — a bank which had already turned the doctors down.

The meeting that Wednesday afternoon was the first of several. There were visits to the architect and to the building contractor. Bids were reviewed. Alleman made several suggestions, quite sensible ones, for changes in the plans. When he decided that he was satisfied, he announced that he would back the medical group with a letter of credit in the amount of $1,500,000. In return, he would collect from the assembled physicians a check in the amount of $50,000.

The letter of credit on the letterhad of the J.P.A. Corporation did not immediately convince the loan officer at the bank that Alleman was good for that much money. He checked out Alleman. Alleman had not been in the city long, but he was able to display stunning assets. He had stocks and bonds beyond the dreams of avarice. His books had recently been audited by a local firm of public accountants, and the audit was impressive. He displayed his Dun & Bradstreet rating.

Reassured, the bank advanced to the doctors part of the money required to construct their building. The building contractor excavated the foundation, and the first concrete was poured.

Suddenly, Alleman was seen no more. He disappeared into thin air, abandoning his handsome office and his secretary and taking with him that glowing audit and the impressive array of stocks.

The doctors were left with a hole in the ground.

The bank was left with a letter of credit which was good only as scratch paper.

Alleman was, of course, a con man, and his company was a dummy company. The setup was typical — the properly furnished office, the books, the audit, and a safe full of stolen or borrowed or forged stock.

In bilking the bank, Alleman ran afoul of federal law. Word went out to federal offices all across the country and to bank officers. Two months later, when a group of eight professional men, including two lawyers, presented a letter of credit from the

Charles Dunham Corporation to a bank in Ohio, the loan officer acted with caution. No one likes to offend a wealthy man. However, the professional men were seeking a loan for the purpose of building an apartment complex, and the case was curiously similar to the Allemann affair.

Federal investigators also acted with caution, and they discovered that the president of the Charles Dunham Corporation looked exactly like J. P. Alleman. They had a photograph of Alleman, snapped without his knowledge at a country club affair.

Charles Dunham and J. P. Alleman were one and the same person, and that person had no assets at all.

How can a con artist convince everyone, including Dun & Bradstreet, that he is a financier with tremendous wealth?

According to David P. Curnow of the U.S. Attorney's Office in San Diego, and formerly Chief of the Fraud and Special Prosecutions Section of the U.S. Attorney's Office in Los Angeles, it is not very difficult.

First of all, there is the fact that all business is to some extent based on trust. That's the way the world operates.

The flim-flam man employs a local firm of auditors to go over his books and to examine his stocks. The con man is the client, and the auditors may not wish to lose the account. If some press too hard, insist too strongly that they must verify the validity of the securities, the con man may become testy and threaten to dismiss them and employ another firm for the audit. Some auditors are especially wary of lending their names to clients who may possibly be swindlers, and these firms are usually avoided by the con artist.

The audit and the presence of apparent assets are, of course, all that can be reported by Dun & Bradstreet.

In the Alleman case, the loan officer could have saved himself, his bank and his group of doctors a great deal of grief if he had not been so easily convinced by the audit and the apparent assets of the accomplished con man. Like everyone else in the world, the federal government agencies responsible for the investigation of frauds have become computerized. In Washington, D.C., the Securities and Exchange Commission maintains a computer bank with information about every schemer who has come to the attention of the securities industry. Anyone with a legitimate business interest has access to this computer, and Alleman was an old pro. Under several aliases, he had pulled the advanced fee swindle in a number of states.

Even if Alleman had been a gifted newcomer to the field of fraud, the bank officer might have contacted the F.B.I., which has accounting squads made up, for the most part, of C.P.A.'s. These squads audit federal banks, and they also audit private business-men who are suspected of participating in frauds that violate federal statutes.

Had he been averse to calling in the F.B.I., the bank officer might, not unreasonably, have insisted on verifying the authenticity of Alleman's securities himself.

The nation's business does operate because we trust one another, but unless he deals only with well-known and long-established firms, the loan officer can be taken by a con artist if he doesn't exercise care and vigilance.

Chapter 11

SOMETIMES A CIVIL SUIT IS THE ANSWER — AND SOMETIMES IT IS NOT THE ONLY ANSWER

THE businessman or the consumer who is neither greedy, unscrupulous or careless can be badly taken by confidence men who operate in what seems to be a perfectly normal manner, but then simply fail to meet their obligations.

THE CONFIDENCE MAN BELIEVES THAT THE WORST THING THAT WILL HAPPEN TO HIM WILL BE A CIVIL SUIT, AND OFTEN HE IS RIGHT. Mr. Gerald Harrison, a midwesterner who dealt in poultry, conducted his business with diligence and always checked the credit rating of people who ordered from him before making a shipment.

When Mr. Harrison received an order from the firm of Bigelow and Ferguson (not the actual name) he did what he usually did. He ran a credit check. The firm, he learned, was a partnership, newly formed, with offices in Los Angeles. The partners, James Bigelow and Charles Ferguson, had an account in a Los Angeles bank in the amount of $5,000. Satisfied, Mr. Harrison shipped Bigelow and Ferguson the frozen chicken parts they had ordered. Two days later his bookkeeper sent an invoice to Bigelow and Ferguson. The invoice, in the amount of $450, was paid by return mail. On the day Harrison received the check from Bigelow and Ferguson, he also received a telephone call. Bigelow and Ferguson urgently needed several hundred pounds of frozen chicken necks and backs.

Mr. Harrison was pleased, since few things appeal more to a poultry dealer than good customers who order lots and lots of frozen chicken parts. He hurried the shipment on its way and again his bookkeeper sent an invoice to Bigelow and Ferguson.

This second invoice was not paid for three weeks, which is not unusual. Payment within ninety days is considered standard.

In the interim, Harrison received several more telephone orders for frozen chicken parts, and he promptly filled the orders and sent the chicken to Los Angeles.

At the end of a month, Harrison had been paid for two shipments of frozen chicken parts, and he had actually filled ten orders from Bigelow and Ferguson. Mr. Ferguson, in the course of one telephone conversation, apologized for the slight delay in sending payment on several of the Harrison invoices and told Mr. Harrison that he was behind on his paperwork but that payment would be forthcoming.

Mr. Harrison did not feel uneasy, and he continued to ship chicken to Bigelow and Ferguson in Los Angeles.

At the end of three months, Mr. Harrison was extremely uneasy. Bigelow and Ferguson were into him for a quarter of a million dollars worth of frozen chicken; and Harrison, not a millionaire himself, was beginning to have difficulty meeting his own bills. He began to dun Bigelow and Ferguson.

What he got was promises and also a few excuses and no money.

He threatened to retain an attorney in Los Angeles.

Bigelow and Ferguson made still more excuses.

Harrison did retain an attorney in Los Angeles. His attorney met, out of court, with the attorney who had been retained by Bigelow and Ferguson. The meeting was amicable, and there were more promises but no payment.

Harrison's attorney filed a civil suit against Bigelow and Ferguson, and of course obtained a judgment against the partners since they certainly did owe Mr. Harrison for tons and tons of chicken.

Bigelow and Ferguson accepted the judgment and did not appeal, file bankruptcy, or take any legal action to avoid paying Harrison. They simply dissolved their partnership, closed their office, and went on a holiday.

In many cases, both Harrison and his attorney would have assumed that they had a purely civil matter on their hands and might have gone on for years trying to collect their money and not collecting it. Mr. Harrison, however, was a man who did not like being taken. Bigelow and Ferguson had made off with a large hunk of his inventory. Harrison was angry, insulted, embarrassed, and also short of capital as a result of their venture into the frozen chicken business. Harrison called several law enforcement agencies and was finally advised to contact the United States Attorney's Office, since Bigelow and Ferguson had used the mails and had also used the telephone and telegrams to deprive Harrison of his property. There is a wire fraud statute, a spin-off of the mail fraud statute, which gives the federal government jurisdiction in a fraud situation where interstate communications systems are used.

MR. HARRISON, UNLIKE MANY VICTIMS OF FRAUD, WAS NOT SATISFIED TO STOP WITH A CIVIL CASE; HE WAS OUT FOR BLOOD AND HE GOT IT. The Fraud Division of the U.S. Attorney's Office in Los Angeles was alerted. The investigators in Los Angeles were well up on the statutes and case law, and they had equipment and facilities which were not available to Harrison or to his private attorney. They began a rundown on James Bigelow and Charles Ferguson. They discovered that these two gentlemen had an interesting manner of conducting business.

Two years before they formed their partnership and began ordering frozen chicken from Harrison, they had been dealers (under the name B&F Commodities) in frozen fish. They had ordered quantities of frozen fish from a firm in New England, had paid the invoices on the first two shipments of fish, then had stalled further payments. The New England firm had engaged a lawyer and obtained a judgment against them. They had then ignored the judgement.

The New England firm which shipped frozen fish to Los Angeles had been unable to collect on the judgment. They had eventually given up trying to collect and had not attempted to bring criminal charges against Bigelow and Ferguson. They had absorbed their losses.

The year following the frozen fish venture, they had gone into the dog food business. They had ordered quantities of the components which go into dog food, had paid for the first one or two orders, then failed to make further payments. The suppliers of dog food had brought civil suits against them, had obtained judgments, and then had not been able to collect on these judgments.

"What these two were doing," explains David Curnow, of the

U.S. Attorney's Office, "was first lulling the suppliers into a false sense of security by promptly paying on the initial orders. They then ordered increasingly larger quantities of a commodity. The commodity market moves quickly. Once a shipment was on the way, they would run to another distributor of fish or dog food or whatever and sell the shipment at a discount — way below the market price, so that it couldn't help but move. They'd collect their money fast, saying they were short of cash and needed the money to meet their obligations.

"The two relied on the fact that frozen fish people probably don't know much about dog food, and a poultry man isn't likely to contact a supplier of fish.

"They stepped up the pace of their operations, figuring that they could stay in business for a few months at a time, could fend off their creditors, could then have their attorney meet with the creditors' attorneys, could promise to pay, could accept the civil judgment when it was finally entered against them, and then could simply walk away from that judgment.

"They didn't even bother to move or to change their names. They like the climate in California."

The two con artists were, for a time, removed from the climate they so enjoyed, and they went to prison.

Had it not been for the irate Mr. Harrison, they might have been back in the commodities market the next year peddling ham or apples.

THIS SORT OF SWINDLE, THE SIMPLE NONPAYMENT OF BILLS, IS NOT CONFINED TO THE COMMODITIES MARKET. IGNORING A CIVIL JUDGMENT IS A COMMON THING, AND USUALLY THE PERSON WHO HAS BEEN SWINDLED, WHO HASN'T RECEIVED THE MERCHANDISE HE ORDERED OR WHO HASN'T RECEIVED PAYMENT FOR SERVICES OR GOODS SUPPLIED, WILL GIVE UP AFTER A TIME AND WRITE OFF HIS LOSS. In the Harrison case, the accumulation of data by the federal investigators clearly showed fraud — criminal fraud.

The con artists had their scheme well worked out, and they could have gone on forever, except for one angry man. Once the report was made — the report which started the investigation by federal agents — the repetition of a deliberate criminal pattern became clear.

The con men had repeatedly delayed payment and had repeatedly made false statements about the delayed payments. They had promised that the money would be forthcoming. After three years and three different ventures into commodities, it would be ridiculous to believe that they ever intended to pay for those shipments of frozen fish, chicken parts and dog food.

It would be ridiculous to believe that they ever intended to comply with any of the civil judgments against them.

THE INVESTIGATOR WHO HAS JURISDICTION IN ANY CASE CANNOT KNOW OF THE EXISTENCE OF A FRAUD IF HE DOESN'T GET A REPORT. TOO OFTEN, THE PRIVATE LAWYER DOESN'T MAKE A REPORT OR DOESN'T URGE HIS CLIENT TO MAKE A REPORT. HE HASN'T THE TIME AND HE DOESN'T REALIZE THAT HE'S DEALING WITH SWINDLERS. Again, a public information program is essential.

Private attorneys and injured individuals should be encouraged to communicate with officialdom, no matter how embarrassing that communication may be.

THE CASE OF THE ROMANTIC COMPUTER IS ONE EXAMPLE. Computers are not, of themselves, romantic. They have marvelous memories and can feed back whatever information is given them quite quickly. However, computers cannot manufacture people, and they cannot inform anyone of anything that has not already been fed into them.

We will forget, for the moment, that they sometimes foul up people's telephone bills. We will bow low before the computer and decide that it is the operator who really fouled up the bill, and the computer at the telephone company only reproduced information that was faulty to begin with.

If one can prove that a person is intentionally channeling faulty information into a computer, interesting things may happen.

For a time the computer became a matchmaker. Single girls paid fifteen dollars or so to have their names inserted into a computer, which would then match them with a single man who had paid fifteen dollars or so because he wanted to meet some nice single girls. The computer could deliver to a young woman a man who was six feet tall (provided such a one had registered with the computer dating service), who liked to dance, and who was a Presbyterian (if that was what she had requested). The computer could deliver to a young man a girl who was blonde and did not weigh two hundred pounds, provided that a reasonably slim blonde had registered with the computer dating service.

So far so good. For young men and women, or even older men and women, the computer dating service was the answer to a problem. Men and women could meet one another without resorting to single bars or joining Parents without Partners.

Then, in at least one case, the sharpies moved in. No doubt in several cases the sharpies moved in. The con man who got nailed in this particular case history was a man with a beautiful and personable wife, a spotty history of employment, and access to a computer.

Anyone can have access to a computer. One needs only to contact a firm which rents computer time and arrange for a certain number of "runs" per month.

This man, whom we will call Henry Anderson, went into the matchmaking business in style. He rented a suite of offices in an extremely posh neighborhood, called in a decorator, and had the offices furnished in impeccable style. He engaged a psychologist to evaluate the personalities and possible hangups of his clients and he advertised.

What did he advertise?

He advertised that his service offered the best. He advertised that the men who came to him seeking female companionship were doctors, lawyers, chemists, engineers. They were also handsome, intensely personable, popular already, and not ugly. Never ugly. Never fat.

He advertised that the women who came to him seeking male companionship were intelligent, beautiful, svelt, and already so entrancing to the opposite sex that they were beating off suitors with a baseball bat.

Henry Anderson not only advertised, he charged a great deal of money for his computer matchmaking. He was not in the fifteen dollar class. A thousand dollars, paid in installments, was not unusual.

Anderson also sold his paper immediately to a finance company

— a company which supposedly was completely independent of his dating service, but which was actually owned by his beautiful wife and his brother-in-law.

Could Henry Anderson deliver on his advertised promises? Could his computer introduce svelt, charming girls to bright young doctors and lawyers? Could it insure "compatibility" through the services of his psychologist?

No, it could not. Svelt, charming girls did not register with the dating service, since they did not need it. A svelt, charming girl can get a date very easily. The world teems with men who lust after such morsels of femininity.

Bright, handsome young doctors and lawyers also can do without the computer matchmaker. Handsome young doctors often marry pretty nurses and lawyers may marry their secretaries or perhaps lady lawyers, but they are generally not lonely.

What Henry Anderson did, through his computer, was to introduce unattractive truck drivers to hopeful waitresses. Girls who hoped for a bright whirl with a debonair man found themselves having coffee with a glorified file clerk at a corner cafeteria.

Does anyone need to pay $1,000 for this?

The clients began to sue. And sue and sue. Then several complained to the District Attorney. The stories were drearily similar, and it was plain that Henry Anderson had been lying. He did not have doctors and lawyers and "beautiful" people in his files.

When the matter of Henry Anderson was brought to the attention of the District Attorney, a civil suit was started against Anderson.

As of this writing, the suit has not yet been settled. "What usually happens," said a spokesman for the District Attorney, "is that the suit will be settled out of court. The man probably will not go to jail, which is rather a shame, but we may be able to recover some of the money his clients spent. Also, we have been able to give the case enough publicity to put him out of business. He won't be able to swindle any more widows, spinsters and bachelors — until he thinks up another gimmick."

IF ALL ELSE FAILS, THE INJURED PARTY HAS ONE GOOD CHANCE OF GETTING SOMETHING BACK ON A BAD INVESTMENT. HE CAN TIP OFF THE INTERNAL REVENUE SERVICE. The IRS is not the most loved institution in the United States, and most citizens have a horror of being squealers. However, the person who has been victimized by a con man may suspect that if the con man cheated him, he might also cheat Uncle Sam. He may walk away from a civil judgment, hide his assets in a dummy corporation; but, unless he fades into obscurity or leaves for Mexico, he will have trouble hiding from the Internal Revenue Service. And the person who informs on the income tax cheat does get part of the money the IRS is able to collect because of the tip.

Chapter 12

SAFE AS A BANK IS NOT THAT SAFE

IN films and on television, people who want to rob banks provide themselves with guns, masks and, occasionally, high explosives. It's a simple and direct approach, and so easy to understand that even little old ladies try it.

The trouble with using a gun is that someone is apt to get hurt. Con artists have no desire to get hurt and they can use a sweet, innocent smile, a few forged documents, and a bit of time to rob banks safely.

A FAVORITE METHOD IS BY KITING: RAISING THE VALUE OF AN ACCOUNT BY DEPOSITING CHECKS, SOME OF WHICH ARE VALUABLE ONLY AS WALLPAPER. Miss Natalie Johnson, who looked like everybody's favorite maiden aunt, opened a checking account at a suburban branch of the Nashville Merchants and Traders Bank with a deposit of $150, which was made in cash. For a few weeks, Miss Johnson made similar small deposits and wrote modest checks to cover such necessary items as gas at her nearby flat, electricity, a new dress at the local department store, and groceries. Many of her deposits were made by mail.

After Miss Johnson had her little bank account running smoothly, she visited the branch bank to inform the manager that she was taking a trip to visit a nephew in Chicago. She would, she said, retain her little apartment, since one does need a place to come home to. However, she requested temporary change of address on her account. The manager was happy to see to the matter, and Miss Johnson wrote a larger check payable to an airline and departed from Nashville.

Three days later, at a branch bank in one of the more prosperous suburbs north of Chicago, Miss Harriet Underwood appeared at the desk which handled new accounts and filled out an application for a checking account.

"I'm opening a needlework shop on Main Street," she told the woman who presided over new accounts. "I think the checks should be imprinted with the name of the shop. My nephew says it will be more businesslike, and I can keep things straight for the tax people."

The new accounts lady hid a smile. Miss Harriet Underwood had a fuzzy, absent-minded air, a cluttered handbag, and a way of squinting at the application form that indicated she badly needed to wear her bifocals but was probably too vain to succumb to this need.

The new accounts lady suggested that Miss Underwood might wish to open a business account in the name of Harriet's Needlework, and a personal checking account in Miss Underwood's own name.

Miss Underwood considered this, then decided against it. "I won't need a personal account," she announced. "I'll just pay myself a salary every week out of the shop account; that will cover everything I need."

The new accounts woman did not press the matter. Miss Underwood presented for identification an Illinois driver's license, a social security card, and, touchingly, a baptismal certificate.

Within a week, Harriet's Needlework shop did open on Main Street, and Miss Underwood presided over the place in a ladylike way and sold yarn, canvas and needles to the ladies of the town.

A few days after the shop opened, the Nashville bank received a check from Harriet's Needlework shop to be deposited to the account of Natalie Johnson.

A few days after that the Illinois bank accepted a deposit from Harriet's Needlework shop which included several checks from ladies in the town, some cash and a check drawn on the Nashville bank and signed by Natalie Johnson.

A day or so later the Nashville bank received another check from Harriet's Needlework shop and credited it to Natalie Johnson's account.

In the months following, more deposits were mailed from Illinois to Nashville. Included in these deposits were checks from Harriet's Needlework shop. The Nashville account showed a higher and higher balance.

At the same time, more deposits were made in the Illinois bank, and these were comprised, in part, of checks written by Natalie

Johnson on the Nashville bank. The balance credited to Harriet's Needlework shop by the Illinois bank soared.

After four months, Miss Underwood appeared in the branch office of that Illinois bank and announced that there had been an emergency in her family. She needed cash, and lots of it. She needed, in fact, $150,000.

She did not get $150,000 in cash. Few branch banks have this kind of money in their vaults. Miss Underwood did, however, receive a cashier's check in the amount of $150,000. There was no trouble about that at all. The records showed that she had almost $200,000 in her account.

Miss Underwood accepted the cashier's check and took the commuter train into Chicago, where she went directly to the main office of the bank.

At the main office, she asked to speak to one of the bank officers. She presented the cashier's check to a vice president of the bank and asked for $150,000 in cash in bills of large denominations. Miss Underwood had all her proper identification, including her baptismal certificate.

The vice president advised her against carrying that much cash and, when she insisted, he called the branch in that suburb where she had her account. The manager of the branch assured the vice president that the cashier's check was genuine and that there were ample funds in Miss Underwood's account to cover the withdrawal.

Two days later there was horror in both Nashville and Chicago as checks began to bounce.

Miss Harriet Underwood of Harriet's Needlework shop and Miss Natalie Johnson were, of course, one and the same person. What Miss Underwood/Johnson had done was reasonably simple, but required close attention and a keen talent for timing and bookkeeping.

First, Miss Underwood/Johnson opened the account in Nashville with a modest deposit and ran the account for a brief time with additional deposits of good checks and cash. Then she departed for Illinois.

Once established in Illinois, she beefed up the Nashville account with checks written on the Illinois bank — checks that were not covered by the funds she had on deposit in Illinois.

Before the checks she sent to Nashville could clear through to Illinois, she boosted the amount credited to her Illinois account by depositing checks from the Nashville bank.

She had sent checks back and forth from one state to another until it appeared that the new worth of Harriet's Needlework shop stood at more than $200,000 — if one looked only at the tabulations on the card which showed her banking transactions.

In fact, the amount of good money, real checks from real people, which had been paid into the two accounts amounted to less than $30,000.

With two days head start, Miss Underwood/Johnson disappeared and, as of this writing, she has not been seen again. Perhaps she is now in some other town with another small business and another pair of bank accounts and she may be hiking the amounts with fictitious checks.

She may be caught, but if she keeps abreast of banking procedures and keeps her sense of timing, she probably will not be caught.

WHY WILL SHE NOT BE CAUGHT? Because, sadly enough, some bank officers (and tellers, branch managers, etc.) do not wonder mightily at odd things. In the case of Miss Underwood/Johnson, no one wondered that a needlework shop on Main Street was pulling in that kind of money.

Probably the all-time champion of check kiters is a middle-aged woman who had an account in a Georgia bank and one in a branch bank on Los Angeles' Wilshire Boulevard and who succeeded in walking off with nearly half a million dollars. It took her ten months to pull this caper and her cover was a small office on Wilshire where she sold hosiery distributorships.

She may well be in Hawaii today, enjoying the sunshine.

KITING IS NOT THE ONLY WAY A BANK CAN BE TAKEN; THERE ARE HUNDREDS OF VARIATIONS, AND BY THE TIME THIS BOOK REACHES PRINT, THERE MAY BE THOUSANDS. Consider the well-dressed and charming businessman who presents himself to the bank officer in charge of new accounts and opens an account with a large check drawn on an out-of-state bank.

The man is indeed charming because that is how he makes his

living, on charm. He is witty and debonair and he tells the bank officer some clever stories; and he also invites the bank officer to lunch (at a very good restaurant) and asks his advice on several matters. He wants to open an office; does the bank officer know of a good business building which might have a vacancy?

He is considering buying a home. Which would be the best part of town to look for a residence? He has to consider the school districts. He has children.

The banker is as helpful as he can be; it is the business of bankers to be helpful, to build new accounts. The man's superiors will be delighted to have this impressive person's money in their vaults.

In a very few days, perhaps as long as a week, the banker is practically in the con artist's pocket. Although the check on the out-of-town bank may not have cleared, the affluent con man is writing checks on his new account. He is buying things — valuable things. Perhaps a car, bonds, stocks, furniture. Sometimes he mutilates his checks so that the computer will kick them out and they will have to be sorted by hand. Sometimes he has compromised the hopeful banker so completely that the banker can be induced to hold back the checks so that they won't clear. "I have more money coming in from out of state," the con man will explain. "It'll be here in a few days. Don't let that check to Wilfred Cadaillac go through."

Compared to a really ingenious kiting scheme, this sort of thing is over quickly. The con man will only work it for two or three weeks, just long enough for him to unload his new car, his stocks and his new furniture for cash and to disappear; at which point the out-of-state check is bounced, and all the local checks begin to bounce and the roof falls in on the poor bank officer who covered for the crook.

Which, perhaps, is only justice. But then, few of us breathe who can't be taken in by a good flim-flam man.

NOT ALL SWINDLERS HAVE TO BE CHARMERS. One con man opened five separate ccounts in five separate branches of one bank. The accounts were all under different names, and were all in amounts totaling nearly $2,000. There was no hanky-panky about out-of-state funds and no need to take a bank officer to lunch. These accounts were opened with real money, and they were as good as gold.

The con man wrote a few checks on his various accounts so that they would appear to be normal, active accounts.

He waited a few weeks. He waited for a Thursday, since Thursday was payday for most industries and businesses in the area. Banks remained open until six on Thursday evenings and the lines at the tellers windows were long. The tellers were rushed and, in spite of warnings to think only of one customer at a time, they tended to be harrassed and upset.

On a Thursday afternoon, the con man inserted himself into the crowded lobby of a branch where he had an account amounting to $1,862. He waited patiently until it was his turn to do business with a teller. He handed the teller a check for $1,623. She quickly checked his card, and, assured that the check was good, she counted out the money, made a quick notation on a pad, and slipped his check into her cash drawer.

In the rush, she did not put a notice on his card to hold further withdrawals.

Satisfied, the man melted into the crowd. He attached himself to the end of the line of customers and waited patiently and reached the window of another teller. He then presented a check for the balance of his account. The teller looked at his card, noted that at the moment his account stood at $1,862, and handed him that amount.

He left the branch, hurried to a second branch, and repeated the operation.

Half an hour later, he was at a third branch, and then hurried to a fourth and then to a fifth branch. In one afternoon, he bilked the bank of nearly ten thousand dollars. He departed from the fifth branch only fifteen minutes ahead of the warning telephone call from the main office.

True, it took him a few weeks to set the whole scheme up, but ten thousand dollars is not bad money for a few weeks work, and he didn't have to work hard.

THERE ARE QUICKER, EASIER AND SAFER WAYS TO DO IT. Con artists dearly love to get their hands on bank mail. In the old days, they used to buy bank trash. One bunco cop told the authors of a man who paid janitors three dollars a sack for bank trash, and the investment was handsomely rewarded.

All the con man had to get was a bank document, perhaps a deposit slip which a customer had goofed and then tossed into a wastepaper basket. With this in hand the con knew what he needed to know about the depositor, he knew the number of his account and under what name the account was carried by the bank. Armed with this information, he could telephone to the statement department of the bank, give the name and account number, and be informed of the amount on deposit.

He could then forge bank checks and proceed to clean out the account. The depositor would have no way of knowing that his funds were being stolen until his own checks started bouncing.

Today most banks shred their trash, and an open wastepaper basket in the lobby of a bank is a rarity. Customers who make mistakes on deposit slips or checks do not tear up the deposit slips and drop them into the wastepaper basket because the banks thoughtfully provide sealed receptacles for waste. There is, however, still the United States Postal Service.

One gang of real pros cruises cities on the West Coast. They will case an area until they find an apartment house, preferably one in an upper-middle-class neighborhood, which has a letter box which can be opened by a master key. The master key is in the possession of the mailman on the route, but this does not deter the crooks. Among their number is a locksmith.

The cons pop the master lock on the letter box and make off with it for a brief time — long enough for their locksmith to make a key which will fit the box.

The lock is then restored to the apartment house box. With any luck at all, no one will have noticed its absence.

For several weeks, nothing happens, and no one is aware that a key to the master lock exists and is in the hands of criminals.

But that key can open post boxes anywhere on the route. The gang can open the box down at the corner or over on the next block and riffle through the envelopes and pull any that might contain checks, deposits, passbooks or other bank documents.

With modern offset printing, it is no problem for the bunco artists to print up whole books of checks and then, as outlined above, to loot the local depositors. Checks are usually cashed at branches of a bank where a depositor does not have an account. Identification in the form of driver's licenses, credit cards and the like can be easily forged. Even the signatures will match pretty well the signatures on the depositors' own checks.

As the postal people became aware of this scheme, they began replacing locks. In many areas the master key which unlocks the apartment house drop box will no longer unlock the letter box at the corner. The postman has to carry two different keys.

"It doesn't make a lot of difference, though," said one postman sadly. "Not everybody's so refined about stealing mail. Some guys just use a screwdriver to get into the corner boxes. Some guys swipe the mail sacks off the trucks, and they don't mind roughing up a mailman to do it. Me, I won't ride a post office truck. I use my own car to haul the mail from the post office to my route, and I won't put any notice on it so anybody will know there's mail in it. I have trouble parking, sometimes, but I'd rather get a ticket than get dead and I don't want to lose any mail."

STOLEN, LOST OR FORGED CREDIT CARDS ARE A BANKER'S NIGHT-MARE. The credit card is such a convenience to the legitimate businessman that it will probably always be with us. As more and more bank cards have been issued, however, and lines of credit amounting to a thousand or two thousand dollars have been granted even to depositors of modest means, the crooks moved in and had a field day.

The banks have fought back. Everyone who issues credit cards maintains a "hot list" — a list of the numbers of stolen or lost cards. Card holders are encouraged to keep a record of their account numbers and to report to the lending institution the moment they are aware that a credit card is lost. Most cards are renewable annually, and after the cards are mailed to the users, banks can follow up within a week or ten days with a letter to the customer asking whether he has indeed received his card.

Branch banks and merchants who accept the cards in lieu of cash are encouraged to check the hot lists, and in some high risk areas there are computer terminals where a retail clerk or a teller can punch the number of a credit card into the computer to see if it is a stolen or lost card.

The professional frauds who use stolen cards are onto the tricks. They usually dress well, don't try to buy things that are too expensive (the purchase of a silverplated bowl which retails at $15.00 will not be so carefully examined as the purchase of a stereo sound system which is tagged at $150.00). If a clerk disappears into a stock room or behind a desk to check the card number, the crook will not linger.

Usually the frauds have access to the hot lists, too. As soon as a card number shows up on the lists, the con man will discard it and start working with a new card.

If the crooks are able to corrupt local merchants, they can have a merry time without worrying about hot lists.

The Miami police reported on a ring in operation in that city which made off with more than $5,000 in cash and merchandise every week. Both male and female operatives used stolen credit cards, which they presented to "cooperative" merchants. Sometimes the thieves and those accommodating retailers did not even go through the motions of handing merchandise over a counter. The merchants simply wrote up charge slips for rather large amounts, and split the cash fifty-fifty with users of the hot cards.

For large "purchases," those in amounts up to and above $200, the ring used cards which had been stolen from the mails or obtained in such a way that the legitimate owner would not be likely to miss the card for several days. The merchant could then telephone in to the issuing agency and get authorization to make the "sale" to the "customer."

The members of the ring were nabbed and the "cooperative merchants" were identified when Miami detectives arranged with Master Charge and BankAmericard officials to set up two dummy accounts and issue two cards with the minimum credit line. A plainclothesman then offered to sell the dummy cards to a woman whom he knew to be a member of the ring. The price was reasonable, fifty dollars, and the detective informed the woman that he had swiped the cards from a mailbox. This meant, to the lady con, that the cards were desirable. They would not be likely to show up on the hot list for a week or more.

They did show up on the hot list *immediately*.

Telephone calls from merchants seeking authorization for

large purchases to be charged against the cards revealed the fact that the cards were hot. After those first authorization calls, the cons did not try to charge large amounts against the cards. However, they continued to use the cards for smaller "purchases" with their cooperating merchants. The usual limit for purchases made without special authorization was fifty dollars, and many slips for amounts from ten to forty dollars appeared in the accounts the merchants maintained with Master Charge and BankAmericard people. Those cooperative merchants names appeared again and agin, and the pattern of the fraud and the name of the participants became clear.

It might still have been difficult to prove intent to defraud on the part of the merchants, but it was much easier for the police to put these retailers under surveillance. The police, and the banks, got their break when a twenty-two-year-old girl walked into a men's clothing store and presented one of the hot cards to the manager. A detective from the Miami Police Department stepped up, took the girl into custody, and informed her of her rights.

She was very much aware of her rights, and she wanted to keep them as intact as possible. She did not want to serve a long sentence, and she promptly became a witness for the prosecution.

Her confession involved more than forty retailers in the Miami area, several "creepers" (the thieves who specialize in robbing motel and hotel rooms), a few prostitutes who worked either with creepers or alone to steal cards from their "tricks," and a few down-and-out souls who jimmied mail boxes.

The mastermind who headed this particular credit card ring was taken into custody while he was having dinner at an expensive restaurant. The maitre d'hotel at the place was definitely on the take and permitted customers to charge sumptuous meals on stolen cards. His kickback came in the form of huge tips. The master con, who looked as honest as only a con man can, had a record that included extortion, armed robbery, and carrying a concealed weapon. With the use of the dummy cards, the Miami police were able to add fraud to the list.

EVEN CORPORATE ACCOUNTS CAN BE SUSPECT. A woman in her early thirties came into the main office of a bank in Columbus and identified herself as the corporate secretary for a firm of architects which had offices in Dayton. She had telephoned before coming to the bank and made an appointment with one of the vice presidents, telling him that her firm was planning to open a branch in Columbus. She obtained corporation signature cards from the vice president and opened an account with several checks payable to the Columbus firm. The initial deposit amounted to more than $5,000. She left the bank with the signature cards and, in due time, returned the cards to the bank with the signatures of three principals of the Dayton firm, plus her own signature as corporate secretary. In the months that followed, she regularly deposited checks payable to the Dayton firm in the Columbus bank. As regularly, she withdrew funds from the Columbus bank.

Since the woman was, in fact, an office secretary in the Dayton firm, she was able to maintain good relations with the Columbus bank for several months, and to live high on the hog. What she was doing was simply removing checks from the mail which came into the Dayton office, depositing these checks in the Columbus bank, then removing the money from the Columbus bank and diverting it to her own use. Only a surprise audit (following the complaints of several clients of the Dayton firm) revealed the fact that she was an embezzler. The signatures on the cards she had supplied to the Columbus bank were, of course, forged.

This sort of swindle is possible in small corporations where management controls may not be thorough. However, the Columbus bank was remiss in opening the new account without knowing at least one of the officers of the Dayton corporation. If necessary, a bank officer can visit the office of the corporation to verify that the new account is indeed legitimate; at the very least, a telephone call to the corporation office, plus a check with a bank currently carrying the company's account, should be made.

THE NEW ACCOUNTS DEPARTMENT IS THE FIRST LINE OF DEFENSE IN A BANK, AND UNDER IDEAL CONDITIONS THE PERSONNEL OF THIS DEPARTMENT KNOW THEIR DEPOSITORS AND THEIR ENDORSERS. Ideal conditions rarely exist, especially in large cities. Often it is impossible for bank personnel to know everyone with whom they do business. They should, however, remain alert and keep an eye out for inconsistencies.

In Bakersfield, a shabbily dressed man appeared in one branch bank and announced that he was a newcomer to the town, unemployed, but seeking work, and that he wished to open a checking account. He had four $100 American Express Money Orders which he wished to deposit in the bank.

American Express Money Orders are generally believed to be as good as gold, but the service representative who talked with the man noticed that the addressses on the money orders and the address on the signature card which the man filled out were different. The service representative opened the account, but she saw to it that the man's card did not go into the files. Instead, she reported the transaction to her superiors. A check with American Express revealed that the money orders had been stolen in an armed robbery. A few days after opening his account, the customer returned to the bank and attempted to cash a check for $360.

If the service representative had not been on her toes, he would most surely have succeeded in bilking the bank of that amount. As it was, the police collared the crook before he could even turn away from the teller's window.

BANKS MAY NOT ALWAYS KNOW THEIR DEPOSITORS PERSONALLY, BUT THEY SHOULD KNOW THE MEMBERS OF THEIR STAFFS. Tremendous losses are incurred each year because bank employees go bad.

"There are things you can do with inactive accounts," one bank officer told the authors. "I don't really understand how these accounts can be manipulated, and I don't think I want to understand. If I don't know how to do it, I won't ever be able to do it."

This officer, a woman, did not want to be led into temptation. She will surely have a long and honorable career with her bank and eventually will retire with a clear conscience, a pension and a gold watch.

Not all bank personnel are so pure of heart. Not all can be around money, day after day, week after week, and not succumb to the temptation to let some of it stick to their fingers.

A teller who plays the horses may be a gambler first and a teller second.

A trust officer automatically is a gambler of sorts, since he is responsible for the investment of money entrusted to him; and investments can depreciate as well as appreciate. The trust officer is in an especially vulnerable position since he has at his disposal money for which he may not have to account for years. It may be money held in trust for a minor who will not become of age for ten years or more. It may be money held in trust for the benefit of an incompetent person.

"Suppose the trust officer is in hock," explains David Curnow of the United States Attorney's Office. "What person isn't in hock these days? He owes on a house, a car, maybe on medical bills. Something comes along that looks too good to pass up — a stock that's speculative, but he thinks he can make a killing on it. It's easy for him to dip into a trust fund belonging to a minor and spend it on that stock. If the stock does go up, he can restore the funds. If it falls, he's lost it."

If a trust officer "borrows" from a fund and loses the money, it is the loss of the person in whose name the fund is maintained — unless the bank finds it possible to spread the loss among all trust funds held. The bank can claim that the trust officer acted beyond his authority, which he certainly did. The officer is judgment proof; he doesn't have any money.

Banks Will Never Be Completely Safe, But They Can Be Safer Than They Are. The identity of the customer, and his integrity, should be established before the bank begins transacting business with the customer.

A limited number of people should have access to safes and vaults.

Audits should occur frequently and at unannounced times.

Above all, banks should prosecute when a fraud has been perpetrated. Too many banks are content to let their insurance cover their losses because they don't want the publicity that a criminal prosecution will bring. So long as swindlers and embezzlers are allowed to get away with their crimes, the banks will lose, and so will the depositors.

Chapter 13

THE INVESTMENT SWINDLES

THE late Yellow Kid Weil was the confidence man's con man. He could sell almost anybody anything, and he recognized the fact that the investment business is a gamble — as much of a gamble as putting money on a horse or shooting craps.

In one operation, Weil ran an advertisement in Chicago newspapers announcing that he could take $100 from investors and run it up to $1,000 in no time. Interested parties were invited to write to Simpson and Weil, Bankers and Brokers, at a local address.

When queried by a prospect, Weil asked for an investment of $100 which would be used to place bets on horses. If the prospect really believed that Weil knew more about horses than a jockey, he would part with his $100. Weil then waited a month before mailing a check for $125 to his "investor."

Actually, Weil was not foolish enough to bet on horses. He was using the Ponzi formula, taking money from investors, then paying dividends, so that word of mouth brought in more investors and more money which could be used to pay additional dividends to the original investors and some dividends to later investors.

As the operation continued, the entrance fee went up. Weil started selling stock, and the minimum amount he would accept on a stock sale was $1,000. Weil finally was dealing with four hundred large investors who were so firmly hooked that he was able to take them for almost half a million dollars. When he estimated that he had milked his group for all they were worth, he stopped paying dividends and closed up his "brokerage" and took a long vacation.

The stock market is more closely policed now, and more sophisticated methods are used by the scammers, but the well-intentioned investor can still be taken.

ONE FAVORITE DEVICE OF THE BUNCO MAN WHO SPECIALIZES IN

STOCK SWINDLES IS THE USE OF A SHELL CORPORATION. Norman Teller, a conservative family man with a little money in the bank, was the victim of a classic stock bunk.

Teller did not consider himself a gambler. He didn't care for Las Vegas and he did not play poker. He had a weakness, however; and it was his boat, a twenty-four-foot sloop which he kept in a slip at a marina south of Los Angeles. When he was not working at his building supply business, he was sailing, or caulking, painting, cleaning and fixing his boat.

One day, while he was varnishing the deck of his sloop, he was approached by a man of medium height, a solid and somewhat salty appearing person with graying hair and laugh lines around his blue eyes. The man wore faded denim trousers, an open-necked shirt and nonskid sneakers; he asked if he could come aboard Teller's boat.

"My name's Fred Miller," said the man, "and I saw you talking to Casby the other night."

For an instant Norman Teller couldn't recall who Casby might be. Then he remembered the stocky little man who hung out at the marina bar, which was called Davy Jones Locker, and who claimed that he had a design for a sailing ship that was a radical improvement over all previous designs and that could cut the cost of a sloop by more than half.

Teller smiled. "Casby. Oh, yes, Casby. You a friend of his?"

The man named Fred Miller climbed into the sloop and sat down facing Teller. "I've been checking him out," he told Teller. "Did you know he's working on a design for a new kind of boat?"

Teller nodded. "He says it'll revolutionize the boating world. What's he got in mind? Plastic? That's not exactly new, you know."

"It isn't that simple," said Fred Miller. "Casby's a physicist, did you know that?"

Norman Teller hadn't known that.

"Well, he is," said Miller, "and a group of us have looked at what he's done so far and we have faith in him. We want to back him."

Miller then went on to talk about Casby and the principles involved in the construction of his revolutionary sailboat, and what he said seemed to Norman Teller to make sense. It wasn't simply a matter of a different material for the hull, but of a way of diverting aquatic stresses and strains and making the wind take the pressure of the water so that certain heavy-duty supports and bulkheads would be unnecessary.

"We're having a meeting upstairs in the banquet room at Davy Jones Locker," said Miller at last. "It's at eight-thirty. If you think you might want in on this project, come on over. We'll have eight or ten people there and we'll explain the theory in more detail."

Norman Teller certainly felt that a design which would enable a shipbuilder to turn out a sloop at less than half the cost he had paid would be a real winner, if it were a sound design. That evening, at eight-thirty, Norman Teller was in the banquet room at Davy Jones Locker, together with the physicist named Casby, the newcomer named Fred Miller and several men who also kept boats at the Marina.

Casby said a few words, but he was obviously not a public speaker.

Fred Miller was a splendid speaker. He displayed cutaway drawings, artists' renderings and an organization chart of a newly formed company called Casby Craft. The designs and the artists' renderings looked beautiful to Miller, and the organization chart would have made sense to Norman's daughter, who was then in kindergarten. Only five people were involved in the organization. Fred Miller appeared on the chart as president, and Casby as vice president in Charge of Development. There were three names which Norman Teller did not know.

"We want to begin marketing Casby's idea," said Miller. "We think it will work. We believe in it enough to put our own money into it. We need more, but we don't want anybody's money. We want people who care about the sea and ships.

"We're asking you for $5,000.

"Now this isn't a decision we want tonight. If I sell you hard tonight, tomorrow you'll think you've been conned. If I wait until tomorrow, you'll be sure in your own minds that Casby Craft is something you want to be part of.

"Now we're open for questions on all levels. Casby can handle the technical end, and I'll field any queries on organization and sales."

Norman Teller went home impressed with what he had seen and heard: a new, astonishingly simple and beautiful sailing ship (or at least the design for one); a mock-up of an advertisement which would appear in publications for sportsmen and weekend sailors; cost estimates; bids from suppliers of lumber, fiberglass, canvas; a lease on a building in San Pedro where the actual construction of the Casby Craft would take place. The new company was really organized, very solid.

Also, all original investors had been offered an option to buy the first Casby Crafts at cost.

The next day, when Fred Miller called him at his place of business, Norman Teller announced that he was sold. Two days later Teller had a letter from Miller on Casby Craft stationery asking for a check for $5,000. Teller promptly mailed his check to Casby Craft.

Two months later there was another meeting at Davy Jones Locker and this time there were more men present. Miller showed drawings in more detail, and he reported complete success on this new operation.

"We've been more than successful," said Miller. "We have received prepayments for options on 973 Casby Crafts. Also, along the way we've sold certain patents to other shipbuilders and..."

One of the shareholders interrupted. "Why would you give away our secrets?" he wanted to know.

"We're not giving away anything," said Miller. "We've made certain technological breakthroughs as our engineers got to work, that's all. They have nothing to do with Casby's original concepts. The Casby Craft is still unique. But we were able to sell our technology, so to speak, and for a profit.

"And so, it gives me great pleasure to present each of you with a check for $125. It's not much, I admit, but it does represent a share of our profits which can be distributed without putting any stress on our company."

The investors were delighted to receive their checks, but then they had to confront a problem.

"We've been *too* successful," Fred Miller told them. "We can suspend orders now and be in good shape, or we can continue to accept orders, which means more money for more raw materials.

"We have twenty investors, each of whom has put up $5,000. Tonight I'm asking each of you for $5,000 more. I strongly believe we should expand. I've found out a little about each of you, and I know that none of you will be beggared by another $5,000."

One of the men raised his hand for a question, but Miller stopped him. "Let me finish, please. We'll work it this way: All of you who invested the initial working capital will be given shares of Class A common stock. On that basis you'll continue to receive dividends, just as you have tonight."

"However, those of you who invest $10,000 in Casby Craft will receive certificates for preferred stock. And you'll also receive this!"

With a flourish, Miller opened a box and produced a twelve-inch long model of the Casby Craft. It was a beauty, hand-carved wood with linen sails. "Everyone who invests an additional five thousand will have one of these models with a brass plate bearing the name you select for *your* Casby Craft when it's built."

Norman Teller stared at the model and then closed his eyes and pictured it in his den at home.

The next day he agreed to invest another five thousand in Casby Craft.

He also became a booster. He agreed to talk to his friends about investing in shares of the Class B common stock, and at his urging his best friend put two thousand dollars into the infant company.

In the following two months, Teller saw Casby seldom and Miller not at all. He assumed they were busy selling the new boat and building the prototype, but he did begin to feel a bit uneasy. He finally dialed the number on the Casby Craft letterhead. He got an answering service and he asked that Fred Miller call him at the earliest opportunity.

Three days later Miller returned the call. Miller reported that everything was coming along beautifully, and that the full scale prototype would be completed within a week.

Norman Teller was pleased to hear this. However, after an awkward pause, he came to the real reason for his uneasiness, and for the telephone call.

"I've got ten thousand dollars invested in Casby Craft," he said.

"I'd like something to show for it."

"Well, the first boat will be..." began Miller.

"No," said Teller. "I mean stock. The way I figure it, I'm entitled to five thousand shares of the common at a dollar each and fifty shares of preferred stock at a hundred dollars each. And my friend invested two thousand so..."

Miller laughed. "You're absolutely right. As a matter of fact, several other investors have been asking exactly the same question. You'll have your certificates within a week."

Teller was satisfied, and he did not have to call again. A week later Miller called him.

"Norman?" began Miller. "I'm happy to tell you that the certificates were sent to you registered mail this afternoon."

"Good," said Teller.

"Ah, Norman, this may take some explaining. That's why I'm calling. Our little company has gotten too big. Those of us who are closest to the project decided that to file with the State of California for incorporation would be detrimental to our better interest. We'd have to file blueprints and patent applications and things like that. You know how sticky the state can be. So instead we have merged with Panamint-Apex Corporation. We have, in fact, taken over Panamint-Apex!"

Teller wondered what in the name of heaven Panamint-Apex might be, and Miller informed him that it was a mining concern — an Arizona mining concern. "It hasn't done any business lately, but the corporation is very much alive and beautifully set up. So tomorrow you will have 10,000 shares of Panamint-Apex Corporation stock. You own the mining stock, Panamint-Apex owns Casby Craft, Casby Craft owns the mine. Someday you might even get some raw gold from our private gold mine. How's that sound?"

Teller was not excited at the prospect of gold from a dead mine. He wanted to see the first Casby Craft completed. That was what was important.

"You bet it is," agreed Miller, "and I hope all of our investors are as understanding and farsighted as you are."

The next day the stock certificates arrived, and they looked handsome indeed.

A month went by. The prototype of the Casby Craft was not presented to the shareholders, none of whom was seriously worried. There were always problems and delays when a project as innovative as this was involved.

But then there was a picture of Fred Miller in the newspaper one morning, and an account of Miller's indictment on charges of fraud.

Teller and the other investors quickly met with Casby. They gathered at the bar known as Davy Jones Locker and demanded to know what was up.

"I don't know what's up," admitted Casby. "My design is a good design. Miller took it and helped me develop it, and it'll work, by God! And if we can get that prototype built, I'll prove it to everybody."

This was the first word the investors had had about the prototype in some time. One and all had assumed that it was under construction. But it was not. Casby had been working with Miller, and with a couple of engineers, on refinements, technology, plans. He had visited other groups of investors with Miller. He had seen orders for materials and orders for Casby Crafts. However, the boat had not actually been started. In fact, none of the raw materials had yet been delivered.

The investors in Casby Craft were left holding large amounts of stock in an Arizona mine which had not been worked for twenty years, and which had played out and would never be worked.

"What Fred Miller did," explained a man from the District Attorney's office, "was to look around for an excuse to get people interested in investing. He might have doctored up a pump and presented it to dairymen as a new automatic milking machine that might be marketed. He could have had some pretty drawings made and tried to sell a train that runs without tracks. He could have picked anything. But he decided to go with the boating types.

"He found Casby by accident. Now there was a well-meaning guy with a great idea, except that it wouldn't work. That didn't stop Miller. He used Casby as a springboard. He had a sincere, believable front man. Who could ask for more?

"Using Casby, he found a group of boatmen who could invest.

From the original twenty men, he got a hundred thousand dollars! Once he had them on the hook, he kept playing them.

"He kept Casby pretty well out of circulation. He didn't want Casby talking details with the investors, and also he was using Casby to work the same pitch with members of a yacht club in San Francisco. He got nearly a quarter of a million from them.

"He put a couple of college kids to work on designs and he had a pair of unemployed engineers discussing stresses and stuff with Casby, when Casby wasn't being used to shill for him. He had an artist build that one model that he showed in the meetings, but he never started the full-scale prototype.

"When investors started bugging him about stock certificates, he bought the Panamint-Apex Corporation. He went to Arizona and found a company that owned a musty hole in the ground, and he figured he could hide his boat fraud in that. He got the certificates, and they were as valuable as wallpaper — less valuable. Panamint-Apex was his shell corporation, a corporation that really has no assets.

"It's appalling how many bright, college-educated men put so much faith in printed pieces of paper. That's all those certificates were, paper!"

Norman Teller and the other men who had such faith in Casby Craft never got any of their money back. Miller had spent some money, of course, for that first tiny dividend, for his student designers and artists, for his engineers. He had spent some to buy that worthless mining corporation. He never told whether the rest, which was a considerable amount, went to a numbered account in Switzerland, Rio de Janiero or some other far-flung outpost.

Miller did time for his swindle, and he might have walked away from it before his investors caught on had it not been for the San Francisco boatowner who had invested in the Casby Craft and who had brought his family to Los Angeles on vacation. The man had decided to drop in at the building in San Pedro where the full-scale prototype was under construction and look at the sloop into which he had put so much money.

The San Franciscan had done this, and had seen exactly how much nonactivity was going on. On the day he visited Casby Craft he had found Casby there alone, pouring over still more drawings of the proposed craft, and he had seen immediately that no boat was being built. He had called his lawyer, then hurried to the district attorney's office.

IN THE CASE OF CASBY CRAFT/PANAMINT-APEX, THE SWINDLE WAS THE WORK OF ONE PERSON. AS STOCK SWINDLES GO, IT WAS NOT PARTICULARLY SOPHISTICATED, AND IT DEPENDED TO A GREAT EXTENT ON THE CHARM AND PLAUSIBILITY OF THE SWINDLER. WHEN A GROUP OF CRIMINALS CONSPIRE IN A STOCK SWINDLE, THE POSSIBILITIES ARE ENDLESS, AND CHARM NEED NOT ENTER INTO IT. One group of six men, for example, acquired enough stock in a shell corporation so that they could control the board of directors. In fact, the six swindlers comprised 75 percent of the board. The board, a captive of the swindlers, voted a reverse split which theoretically boosted the value of the stock. Fictitious balance sheets were prepared by a CPA at the direction of the con men, and these further inflated the value of the stock.

The board then voted to issue millions of unregistered, restricted shares of stock; and the defendants then pledged these shares at banks throughout the country and overseas as collateral for loans.

IF THE STOCK IS TO BE USED AS COLLATERAL, OR TO ESTABLISH CREDIT, A SHELL CORPORATION IS UNNECESSARY. STOLEN OR FORGED STOCKS AND BONDS WILL DO NICELY. As we have seen in the advanced fee case in Chapter 10, a stock portfolio often impresses everyone from the local banker to the auditor who draws up the balance sheets for the swindler to Dun & Bradstreet.

Securities, however, are easily transportable and, depending on the security systems in financial institutions, they can be easily stolen. Swindlers can plant confederates in brokerage houses and banks and these plants may be able to flit off with stocks and bonds, which can then be rented to "businessmen" who will ask no awkward questions about the origin of the securities, or which can be used to negotiate loans, or which can be duplicated — endlessly duplicated.

Like the banking documents described in Chapter 12; stocks and bonds can be reproduced by offset printing very easily. To quote Assistant U.S. Attorney David Curnow,

Forgers don't need expensive, hand-engraved plates any

more. They can do their work photographically. The only thing that keeps them from simply grinding out currency is that they can't get the paper. In the case of securities, they don't need the kind of paper that goes to make up ten- and twenty-dollar bills. Practically no one knows what a stock certificate is supposed to look like. Also, even banknote companies, which are licensed to print corporate documents, can be taken in by the scammers. They may conscientiously try to ascertain that the documents they are printing represent a real corporation with real assets, but they, too, can be fooled by the phony audit and the other gimmicks the cons use to make their dummy enterprises appear genuine.

Once the flim-flam man has bogus or stolen stocks in his hands, the possibilties are delightful, for the flim-flam man. He can open accounts with various brokerage houses (using a fictitious name, of course) rent an apartment (using the same fictitious name), establish credit by conducting several small, legitimate transactions with his brokers, then unload his stolen or forged stocks and disappear.

He can borrow money.

He can take advantage of a careless or unscrupulous stockbroker and market his fake stock.

In one case, a scammer appeared at the main office of a large bank and attempted to open an account under a fictitious name. He offered as identification a driver's license and a social security card. The bank officer who checked the paperwork on this new account became suspicious because, while the driver's license seemed perfectly in order, the Social Security card looked too new to belong to a man in his mid-forties. The scammer was invited to wait for a few minutes while some formalities were attended to. The scammer did wait, unconcerned, and the bank officer withdrew to a private office and called the Social Security administration. The Social Security card was a forgery, as was the driver's license, and the scammer's wait was prolonged until the police could arrive to take charge of the new account.

Subsequent investigation showed that the new account had in his possession more than $200,000 worth of stolen bonds, which he planned to market; and it was because of this plan, and only because of this plan, that he needed to open that bank account.

A WORTHLESS COMPANY HAS WORTH TO A CON MAN; A COMPANY WITH SOME APPARENT ASSETS IS EVEN MORE VALUABLE. The shell corporation which was used in the Casby Craft swindle was an admittedly worthless mine. The men who invested in Casby Craft were not interested in mining; they cared about boats.

Promoters with a good spiel can sell stock in worthless companies to investors who *are* interested in mining or oil or whatever.

One con man invited a prospective investor to see an oil well which was a real gusher. The mark made the trip to the site of the supposed oil strike, watched the con man turn a valve and watched black gold pour out of a complicated-appearing pumping apparatus that had been erected at the bottom of a small hill. The sucker happily wrote a check for several hundred shares of stock in the well and the con man drove him home again.

The next day the hustler returned to the site, hooked his pump to a hidden pipeline, and pumped the oil back up the hill to the small storage tank which he had had installed there. He then returned with another prospect, again turned the valve, and again watched oil gush out of his rig.

It was a simple gimmick, but he stayed with it too long. He stayed with it long enough to collect $500,000, but a suspicious investor checked out the operation with an experienced oil man and the subsequent investigation temporarily put the scammer out of the oil business and into prison.

In another oil case, two promoters invited families to a spareribs and beer picnic so that they could admire two brand new wells on the property. The promoters collected money to be invested in the operation of the two wells. The beer and spareribs were real; the wells were only drilling rigs which had been erected the day before the picnic as window dressing. The con men vanished; the rigs still stand. There is no complete record of the day's take for the scammers.

Copper is just as good as gold or oil to a flim-flam man. When the price of copper went up in the United States and people started hoarding pennies, one crook contacted two potential investors and drove them to a hole in the ground where they saw miners hard at work, supposedly digging copper ore. They went to the home of the promoter and studied smelting receipts and they invested. When they had departed, and the crook had cashed their check, the "miners" were ferried back to Skid Row, where they resumed their regular occupation; they were winos, and they were able to stay very high for a few days on the proceeds of their brief careers in the mine.

A paying mine, or industry, is just as good as a nonpaying one, since the con man is saved the trouble of erecting props or hiring fake personnel. One con man purchased a paying mine and sold stock in it — and sold and sold and sold. When, eventually, stockholders received no return on their investment, the SEC moved in. Investors were traced. Testimony brought out the fact that he had sold shares in excess of 38,000 percent of the mine.

NOT ALL CROOKS ARE WHEELERS AND DEALERS WHO LATCH ONTO DEAD MINES OR LIVE INVENTORS. EVEN VERY PRESTIGIOUS AND REPUTABLE FIRMS CAN, UNWITTINGLY, HARBOR AN OPPORTUNIST. "Churning" is the term used in the market for a circular movement of money which can be very confusing to the novice investor, and which can be very lucrative to the unprincipled broker.

In one case, a highly respected firm which we will call Demosthenes and Lucre hired a personable young man to handle new accounts in one of its branch offices. The personable young man handled new accounts very well, and he kept his accounts active. Active accounts are the best kind for a broker, since he makes his money on commissions.

The young man had not been long in his position with Demosthenes and Lucre before he encountered a pair of clients who were the sort of clients any broker dreams of. They were two brothers, once farmers, who had owned large tracts of land in the area and had gone on, year after year, decade after decade, farming that land.

At the time they visited the branch office of Demosthenes and Lucre, they were millionaires. A real estate company had purchased their acres and a housing tract was going up on the land which had once grown beans and radishes, and they had so much money that they didn't know what to do with it. They had been advised by friends to seek the advice of a good, substantial investment firm.

The young broker quickly became very cozy with this pair of instant millionaires. He counseled them, and they began by making a few modest and very sound investments. These appreciated slightly, and at the urging of the young broker they sold at a gain. The broker did not hesitate to point out that this was a much easier way of making money than sowing and watering and reaping, and he encouraged them to make more money faster by trading in more speculative stocks.

In no time they were hooked, just as gamblers are hooked, and at one point their dealings in one speculative stock equaled 50 percent of the volume of trading for the entire nation.

Speculative stocks *are* speculative, however, and some go up quickly and others go down just as quickly. But the young broker continued to collect his commissions on all of the transactions of the two farmers. They sold and bought and sold and bought and checks went from the investment firm to the farmers to the bank which handled the farmers' account and back to the investment firm; and, for a time, the broker was able to get sufficient funds from sales to cover checks to his unwary investors. Eventually, however, the entire system broke down. The investment firm became suspicious of this extremely active account. They had an auditor spend weeks tracing the movement of money and securities and discovered that the two men had lost $500,000. They discovered that the farmers had been persuaded to accept postdated checks from the young broker, had been persuaded to mutilate the checks so that they could not clear through the bank quickly (there was always the chance that their next investment would be a killing and they could recoup their losses); in short, like any gamblers, they had been convinced that the next change in the market, like the next roll of the dice, would put them back in the money.

The two farmers were held responsible by the courts, since they had gone along with the scheme, and the mutilated checks proved that they had. The men were given suspended sentences, and one must admit that they had paid dearly for their excusion into the stock market.

The broker's sentence was *not* suspended. More checking

proved that he had stiffed everybody he had dealt with to some degree. Other customers who were his clients had been taken, although not to the tune of $500,000. Witnesses came forward clamoring for his scalp. The manager at the branch office where he had had his desk was suddenly, possibly rather belatedly, willing to blow the whistle on the opportunist. There was also a cashier who could testify against him, plus another broker in the office who talked to the City Attorney.

In the end, it was the young broker who was the most willing witness against himself. He attempted to murder the cashier. He was a better broker than an assassin, and he failed, but as of this writing he is doing time on a variety of charges.

And the reknowned firm for which he worked? Unofficially they admitted that they might have been remiss in permitting two unknown men and a novice broker in a branch office to trade to such an extent over such a long period of time.

Remiss seems a mild term for it.

Chapter 14

THE INSURANCE SHARPIES

INSURANCE is a game in which everybody can be taken, and insurance swindlers are often not professional scammers. Some are simply individuals who see a chance to collect a spot of unearned money, and who take advantage of it.

THE PRIVATE CITIZEN WHO ISN'T OVERLY SCRUPULOUS MAY LOOK UPON A MINOR AUTOMOBILE ACCIDENT AS A MAJOR BONANZA. A case in point is a young woman whom we will call Loretta. A divorcee with two young children, she works as a secretary in the office of a hardware manufacturer and, because her salary is not sufficient to cover her living expenses, plus baby-sitters for her children, she receives some aid from the state in which she lives. Her children are now old enough, in her opinion, to survive without sitters, and they do not have sitters. However, Loretta continues to collect from the state that extra money which is intended for the care of the children. Loretta spends the money on such necessities of life as color television and electric blenders.

Loretta has learned to play the angles.

One day Loretta was involved in a minor auto accident. It was a rear-end collision which mangled her back bumper and mashed her rear license plate and startled her, but no serious damage was involved. She and the driver of the car which had run into her car exchanged the usual courtesies and Loretta went on her way possessing a slip of paper with the name of the other driver's insurance company.

For three days following this unimportant incident, Loretta appeared in her office as usual and went about her business as usual. On the fourth day, she appeared wearing a surgical collar and complaining of pain in her neck and back. She was, she declared, the victim of a whiplash injury and was under the care of a chiropractor.

Loretta subsequently filed a claim against the driver of the other car for personal injury and mental anguish. As of this writing, her claim has not yet been settled. However, even if one is not equipped with the ability to see into the future, one can safely make several predictions about Loretta.

First, the insurance company will almost certainly compensate her for her "injury." Insurance companies do not like to go into court. Attorneys for insurance companies do not like to face juries composed of citizens who may feel that they have been cheated by an insurance company at one time or another, or who may feel that insurance companies have all the money in the world and there is no reason why Loretta shouldn't have her share. Also, Loretta claims that she is suffering from pains in her neck and back, and it would be impossible for any attorney to prove that she isn't. A whiplash is the favorite injury of accident victims who want to take an insurance company. It is well-nigh impossible to disprove a whiplash.

Secondly, one may predict that once her claim is settled to her satisfaction, Loretta will give up her surgical collar and her visits to the chiropractor will cease. She got along beautifully without that collar for several days following her accident. She must find the thing warm and uncomfortable, and why should she continue to pay money to a chiropractor when she no longer needs one?

Loretta Does Not Consider Herself a Thief, But People Who Don't Mind Being Crooks Can Play the Insurance Game, and the Take Can Be Enormous. A man whom we will call Charles Lewis Forsythe operated an auto body repair shop in a large western city. He was very good at replacing crumpled fenders and banging the dents out of car doors and in time he came to know a great deal about insurance companies which paid him for his work.

Like Loretta, he decided that these companies had pots of money, and that he should get his share.

He wasn't too greedy. He was willing to spread the insurance business around; and he enlisted the aid of a couple of friends who also owned body shops; and they enlisted the aid of friends who owned cars; and they contacted chiropractors who handled many whiplash cases; and they went into the accident business in a big way. Over a period of eighteen months, they made the business pay off to the tune of nearly $100,000.

It would still be paying off today had it not been for one insurance adjustor who noticed that his company was paying an astounding number of claims for accidents following which the cars were repaired at Forsythe's shop, or at the shops of his friends. Many of these accidents involved personal injuries to drivers or passengers, the classic whiplash injuries, and the victims were being treated by chiropractors — four of them who supplied medical reports and bills to substantiate the victims' claims for medical costs and loss of wages.

The insurance investigators were notified, and they contacted the District Attorney and a quiet and thorough investigation was begun.

It took almost a year of dogged, painstaking effort on the part of the investigators, but at the end of that year twenty-one people were indicted on charges of conspiracy, grand theft, forgery, and making false insurance claims.

How did the scammers work?

Forsythe, for one, had obtained several drivers' licenses from the state using fictitious names. He had taken out insurance policies on numbers of cars, sometimes without the knowledge or consent of the owners of the cars. He had then reported fictitious accidents, submitted claims for body work which had not been done, since it is not necessary to repair accident damage when there has not been an accident. He had carefully coached his co-conspirators who were to be the "victims" of the nonaccidents about whiplashes and back injuries, and they had filed claims for loss of wages and for medical costs. These claims were supported by the medical reports of the venal chiropractors whom Forsythe had involved.

Naturally, claims for loss of wages had to be further supported by statements from employers, but Forsythe was equal to this challenge. For him it was scarcely a challenge at all. He simply had the statements typed up on the letterheads of nonexistent companies. Dummy addresses for these companies were set up by a friend.

The chiropractors turned out to be the weak link in the circle of deception which Forsythe had organized. The investigators called upon these men whose reports had appeared so often in the insurance offices, and they took into custody the "sign-in" books, those rosters which are used in almost all medical offices and which a patient signs when he enters the waiting room. The investigators discovered that one patient who had stated that he had visited a particular chiropractor more than twenty times in a three-month period had, in fact, seen the chiropractor only twice.

The patient then had an interview with the men from the District Attorney's office. The man, one of Forsythe's professional victims, did not want to go to prison for insurance fraud. In exchange for a promise of immunity he gladly became a witness for the prosecution, implicating Forsythe as ringleader, his two friends as co-conspirators, plus other professional victims and witnesses to those mythical auto accidents.

Los Angeles County's Deputy District Attorney Barry Sax has handled fraud cases of various types and tries to bring a fresh and unbiased viewpoint to each case. Of insurance frauds, he said, "I tend to blame the insurance companies. When they pay claims without proper investigation, they are wasting *my* money and the money of everybody else who has insurance. The rates go up. If they were a little tougher, a little more careful, a little more suspicious, we wouldn't be paying enormous amounts for auto insurance."

Or, to quote one young man who is, at this writing, training to be an adjuster, "Insurance companies don't really care about what's right; they just seem to care about what's expedient, so they pay the claim."

And then everybody else pays.

THE INSURANCE COMPANIES ARE NOT ALWAYS THE VICTIMS. SOMETIMES THE COMPANIES, OR CERTAIN SALESMEN, ARE CONNING THE CLIENTS. In one bizarre case, an insurance salesman with a flair for big money set out to break all records on sales of huge life insurance policies to wealthy businessmen. He didn't bother with the little folk who might want a $10,000 straight life policy. He wanted the man who could afford a policy for a million or two or three, and he hit upon the perfect gimmick to sell such policies.

"I will pay the premiums for you for the first year," he told his prospects.

Even a millionaire likes to save money, and the premiums on a huge life insurance policy are huge. At first the prospects couldn't believe it.

But it was true. The salesman wrote the policies for his clients, and he did pay the premiums and the policies were as good as gold and the clients were delighted. The insurance company was delighted, and of course paid the salesman big commissions for selling these policies.

Then fantasy set in — the special brand of fantasy which succeeds only when a master scammer is at work. The salesman persuaded the businessman to whom he had sold policies to surrender the policies to him so that he could borrow money on them. The mind boggles, but the policyholders did surrender the policies and the salesman did borrow on them and with the funds he thus gained he sold more policies, collected more commissions, and on and on and on until he was several hundred thousand dollars ahead.

He should have departed for Pango-Pango at that point, since his scheme was basically a Ponzi scheme and he could not go on forever paying premiums out of borrowed money. Perhaps he did intend to depart for Pango-Pango, but he put off his packing a few months too long. Someone at the home office started to pay attention, strict attention, to the brilliant record of this brilliant insurance salesman. That someone decided that no one could sell this much insurance.

The career of the super-salesman was over, and numbers of stunned financiers, factory owners, and leaders of industry had a sticky time trying to explain how they could possibly have been taken in, how they could possibly have been persuaded to hand over their insurance policies so that someone else could borrow on them.

MOST VICTIMS OF INSURANCE FRAUDS ARE NOT BILLIONAIRES; MOST ARE SIMPLE PEOPLE. THEY CAN BE TAKEN IN A VARIETY OF WAYS. The most common swindle is the insurance policy which is so riddled with exceptions and so legalistic in its language that it would take a Ph.D. to figure out how the policyholder is covered, if at all. Very few layman can read insurance policies, and fewer still will be able to make an insuror who writes this kind of policy pay off when the need arises.

It would be difficult, if not impossible, to bring criminal charges against these companies unless it could be proved that there was a consistent pattern of misrepresentation on the part of the salesmen: that the company did, in fact, set out to defraud its policyholders. However, the disgruntled policyholder can have recourse to the agency in his state which licenses insurance companies. All states have such regulatory agencies, and these are in a position to bring pressure to bear on a recalcitrant insuror. If too many complaints build up, the insurance company may lose the right to operate in the state.

Ambulance chasing — that is, soliciting clients for a lawyer — is considered unethical in the legal profession, and in some states it is a crime. However, ambulance chasers do exist, and in some low-income areas the insurance adjuster who arrives to interview the victim of an accident will find that two or three days after the accident the victim has an attorney. "This just isn't normal," said one adjuster. "When the average John Doe has an accident, he doesn't usually run out the next day and get a lawyer. Somebody's getting to these people, telling them they can make money on their accident and taking the cases for a share of the pay-off."

How big a share? Sometimes it can be 100 percent. One human ghoul prowled through hospitals signing up clients. He didn't have to worry about faking medical reports because the clients were truly injured. They had entered the hospitals via the emergency rooms following auto accidents. Their claims were legitimate, and the insurance companies settled the claims with checks payable to lawyer and client jointly. These checks were to be deposited in a trust account for the benefit of the victim. The lawyer was then to make payment to the victim drawing on that trust account.

In many cases, the insurance money got no further than the lawyer's account. Many of the victims received nothing. One woman who had recovered enough to press for payment of her legitimate claim threatened to go to the police. She received payment, a check which bounced. And then she *did* go to the police.

No one can afford not to be insured, and insurance companies really cannot afford to pay on fake claims or to write policies which don't cover the policyholder. The answer to the problem of insurance fraud is, as with banking or the securities business, increased vigilance on the part of the companies, of the agencies which regulate the companies, and cooperation between the private citizen, the law enforcement bodies and the responsible lawyers. Everybody has to pay attention. To quote Barry Sax, "If you have a business where there's a lot of money floating around, and it doesn't seem too hard to get some of that money, somebody's going to try to do it."

Chapter 15

SIMPLY CLIP THE COUPON

THERE is a widely held belief that the bunco man will not try to use the mails to defraud his victims since using the mails to defraud is a federal offense, and the con artist doesn't want to get tangled up with Uncle Sam. In truth, many bunco men do use the mails to defraud, and the Postal Inspectors who try to get their hands on these elusive folk all have stories to tell.

Mrs. Richard Ray, whose given name was Louise, was a bright and cheerful housewife with an unshaken faith in all American institutions. These institutions included all established, well-known, and highly circulated magazines, and the United States Postal Service. She admired the kindly men in blue who carried the mail through snow and sleet and rain and heat. She respected the editors who advised the American public on what to wear, how to cook, and how to treat the common cold.

Mrs. Ray was intrigued by an advertisement which appeared on the inside back cover of her favorite household magazine. The advertisement included a photograph of a handsome middle-aged couple lounging on the warm sands at Waikiki. The copy invited the reader to enroll in the Golden Years Club. The Golden Years Club offered its members many advantages: chances to buy merchandise at discount in member stores, opportunities for low-cost travel on special charter flights, preferred rates at the best resort hotels, and, for continuing membership, special bonuses in the form of sports equipment, gourmet cookbooks and gardening guides.

Mrs. Ray was still on the sunny side of fifty, but the advertisement didn't set down any age limits. The club sounded fantastic, or at least worth investigating, and the magazine in which the ad appeared was so reputable that it was almost sacred.

Besides, there was that coupon. Simply by cutting the coupon out of the magazine and mailing it to the Golden Years Club at a post office box in Pennsylvania, Mrs. Ray would enter a contest.

First prize was a ten-day trip for two to Hawaii. There was no cost and no obligation. The contest was solely to induce prospective members to ask for more information on the club.

Mrs. Ray filled out the coupon, snipped it from the magazine, put it into an envelope, and mailed it to the Golden Years Club at that post office box in Pennsylvania.

Three weeks later, Mrs. Ray received a thrilling letter from the Golden Years Club. She was the winner! Her coupon had been picked from among thousands sent to the club, and she was entitled to the wonderful trip to Hawaii, all expenses paid including air fare. The trip would include a five-day stay in the Royal Hawaiian Hotel on Waikiki, plus a four-day tour of the outer islands, with car and chauffeur supplied on each island.

Mrs. Ray was ecstatic. Her husband was stunned. Mr. Ray did not really believe that anyone won contests. He read the letter from the Golden Years Club with his mouth literally hanging open. In that last paragraph, The Golden Years Club asked Mrs. Ray for thirty-nine dollars "to secure the trip and cover expenses of correspondence."

To Mr. Ray, a free trip was a free trip. Anyone willing to pop for air fare for two to Hawaii, plus five days at a luxury hotel, shouldn't boggle at a few incidental expenses. Why in the name of Hannah did those people want thirty-nine dollars?

Mr. Ray put the question to his wife when she came down to start dinner. "You could write and ask them," she said, "only it would seem kind of chintzy, wouldn't it?"

It would seem chintzy, Mr. Ray conceded. However, he did not sit down and make out a check for thirty-nine dollars. Instead, the next morning he consulted the telephone directory. He made a call. Then he took the magazine with its charming advertisement and the letter informing Mrs. Ray that she was the lucky winner, and he saw the Postal Inspector at the main post office in his city.

The postal inspector examined Mr. Ray's exhibits. He was noncommital, but he asked Mr. Ray to leave the magazine and the letter with him. He advised Mr. Ray not to send any money to the Golden Years Club immediately.

When Mr. Ray left his office, the Inspector wired the main office in Washington.

Ten days later, there were two Inspectors waiting in that small post office in Pennsylvania. There were hundreds of sacks of mail waiting, too, all letters addressed to the Golden Years Club.

When the two men who had rented the post office box for the Golden Years Club showed up to collect their mail, they were gladdened at the sight of those bulging sacks.

Their gladness turned to misery when they confronted the Postal Inspectors and were politely asked to answer a few questions about their club.

"It was a very simple case of fraud," explains David Curnow, Assistant United States Attorney. "Every person who cut the coupon out of the magazine and mailed it in was a winner of the first prize, the trip to Hawaii. Thousands of people were eager to mail their thirty-nine dollars to secure the right to the trip. The men running the fraud just had to wait for the checks to pour into the post office, collect their mail, cash the checks, and disappear.

"If it hadn't been for that suspicious husband, the con men would have been gone long before the protests began to pile up with the postal inspectors. Their outlay was minimal. The display ad in the magazine cost them a few thousand; it cost another few thousand for a mailing service to inform those hordes of 'winners' about the vacation in Hawaii. If they'd gotten away with it, they would have cleared more than half a million dollars."

Mail order fraud goes on at a prodigious rate, but government officials have no way of knowing that a bunco scheme is in operation unless the victims scream. Victims should be encouraged to scream, and should not be made to feel either paranoid or stupid if they suspect they are being victimized.

The "free vacation" bait which Mr. Ray refused to accept is only one mail bunk. It had a certain class because of the medium used for the advertisement and because the advertisement was well-prepared. There are many other common mail frauds.

ACREAGE IN REMOTE COMMUNITIES IS OFTEN OFFERED BY DIRECT MAIL PIECES. These advertisements are usually on good paper, are well-composed and impressive. Some developers offering land this way are perfectly on the up-and-up, but even developers who do not use the mails can be frauds, as we have seen in Chapter

9. A person who considers purchasing land sight-unseen should always, always be discouraged from doing so. If one is bilked and finds out about it quickly enough and complains, law enforcement agencies must move quickly or the land promoters will have fled, changed their names, and probably set up business in another location and composed additional advertisements to peddle additional parcels of worthless lands.

SOME DIRECT-MAIL OPERATORS SPECIALIZE IN STAG FILMS. Direct-mail pieces can be used, or advertisements in the shoddier girlie magazines can give the impression that the vendor of the films has material so hot that it will burn a hole in the postman's satchel. Stag films may not move well in larger, more sophisticated cities where porno movies are shown openly, but in smaller communities such ads can draw customers. What the customer actually receives may be a tepid little short which has nothing going for it but a hot title, or he could receive nothing. The con who placed the advertisement and cashed the customer's check may simply destroy his order and forget it.

Some vendors of "pornographic" material keep operating for comparative long periods of time because the mark who mails the check for the material hesitates to go down to the post office and admit to ordering the stuff.

A GUARANTEED INSECT EXTERMINATOR HAS BEEN A STANDARD MAIL-ORDER FRAUD FOR GENERATIONS. IT STILL WORKS. The dupe who may be experiencing an infestation of ants or roaches spots an ad for this, clips a coupon and sends it, along with his check, to a post office box.

He receives, in return for his two dollars plus mailing costs, a couple of pieces of wood and a piece of paper instructing him to put the insect on one piece of wood, slap the other piece of wood down on the bug and — splat! No more insect.

Can the operator of this dodge be prosecuted? Perhaps, if the victims complain. Few victims complain; the amount involved isn't large enough to fuss about, and the victim feels like a sap.

This is one thing the bunco man relies upon: the victim will feel like a sap. Also, so long as the bite isn't too big, the victim won't yell.

SERVICE TO THE MISSING HEIR IS ANOTHER POPULAR SCHEME.

The operator of this dodge gets his information from the county registrar of deaths. When he finds a person who has died without leaving any heirs and discovers the amount of the estate, he has all he needs. He can comb the telephone books at the public library for the addresses of people with the same last name as the deceased. Shortly, in cities across the nation, people with this name receive a letter pointing out that James M. Soandso died intestate in Suchandsuch County, leaving an estate of $50,000. For a fee, the writer will attempt to establish whether the recipient of the letter is a missing heir.

The amount requested in these letters is reasonable — anywhere from eleven dollars to sixty dollars. Many people are willing to gamble that much in the hopes that they *are* the heirs of the recently deceased James M. Soandso.

Can the operator of this sort of scheme be prosecuted? Perhaps he can. Under the mail fraud laws, the requirements for a guilty verdict are not as rigid as those for other types of crimes. To convict an individual of mail fraud, the government needs only prove that the individual made representations with a reckless indifference as to whether they were true or false. This prevents the defendants from throwing up his hands and saying, "Look, I'm just a terrible businessman and you can't prosecute me for that." While it's true that it isn't criminal to be merely a bad businessman, it may be criminal to act so recklessly that there is no chance that a service will succeed. The mail fraud laws impose upon the businessman the duty to organize and promote a business that has a reasonable chance of success.

One bunco operator who took a whirl at the missing heirs scheme committed a serious error, for which he did time. He found, in the registrar's records, the name of a woman recently deceased. She had died intestate leaving a middling fortune. The delighted con man sent out letters to all the people he could find who had the woman's last name. He did not think two steps ahead; the woman had been married, and he used her married name. Relatives who would have inherited would have had the woman's maiden name. One man who received a letter from the man who was so eager to serve any possible missing heirs spotted the "Mrs." and recognized the ploy. The scheme came to a screeching halt before it had a chance to get off the ground.

FAKE INVOICES ARE RIFE AT THIS TIME, AND FREQUENTLY THEY ARE PAID WITHOUT COMPLAINT. The victim of the fake invoice bunk is the small businessman who is operating with a limited staff and who may not have a system of purchase orders set up. He receives an invoice for advertising in a little throwaway newspaper. It may be a bill with a proof of the advertisement attached, or it may be on a computer card which looks like a telephone bill. An astounding number of people glance at these invoices, okay them, and turn them over to the bookkeeper, or whoever writes the checks for the firm. They aren't sure whether they ordered the advertising or whether they didn't, and they can't take the trouble to find out.

As with all areas of fraud, the best ally the law enforcement agency has is an informed, cooperative public. Again, take the reports, don't make the complainant feel foolish, and watch for the repeating pattern that is the signal that a scammer is in operation.

Chapter 16

IF IT'S "HOT," IT PROBABLY ISN'T EVEN THERE

THE average citizen thinks of a peddler of stolen merchandise as a nasty little man sidling up to strangers on supermarket parking lots, muttering of tremendous bargains, then throwing open his jacket to display a multitude of "stolen" watches pinned to the lining.

The nasty little men with the "hot" watches are still in operation everywhere. The mark who thinks he can get a real buy by bending the law can still do business with them. His chances of actually acquiring a good watch are close to zero. It is possible to manufacture a handsome watch case for very little money. The mark who buys what looks like an expensive watch can find himself with an object encased in phony platinum. It will almost surely cease to work before the mark has had it for two days.

The peddlers of "hot" watches should be approached with a certain amount of caution. If a victim of one of these nasty little men complains to the police and the nasty little man is apprehended, he may calmly display a license which entitles him to peddle schlock watches. No doubt his manner and approach led the mark to believe that the watches were stolen and were expensive, but unless he actually said this to the mark, no charge can be brought against him.

As of This Writing, Things Far Less Portable Than Watches Are Being Peddled as "Hot" Merchandise, and They Are Being Peddled to Some Substantial Citizens of Various Communities. "Smuggled" or "Stolen" Whiskey Is a Staple with Some Cons. Jim Canaday (and that is not his name) was one of the charmed circle in the eastern community where he lived. He had the prettiest wife, one of the bigger houses, one of the best lawns and a huge swimming pool. He was in the advertising business; the big house and the pool were used often and by many.

It paid Canaday to open his home to clients and to the press. His bar bills would have been staggering had he chosen to take his guests to public bars. He did not choose to do this. Instead, he had a houseman who could mix anything from a bloody Mary to a pousse-cafe, and his liquor bills were staggering.

Canaday could not help being interested when he received a telephone call one evening from an anonymous male who claimed he could supply Canaday with twelve cases of Chivas Regal for $500.

"Impossible," said Canaday.

"I've got the stuff, Mr. Canaday," said the caller. "I want to unload it, and none of the regular outlets is interested. They're all worried about their licenses and they've got regular suppliers."

"Is it hot?" demanded Canaday.

"No, it's not hot. It's only that without the duty..."

"It's smuggled," snapped Canaday. "No wonder the regular dealers won't touch it. It hasn't got the stamps."

"Mr. Canaday, your house doesn't get busted," pointed out the caller.

Which was true.

Canaday could write off entertaining on his income tax, but he did not mind saving a dollar, or five, or five hundred. He was a budget-minded man; it was one of the things that had made him a success.

"What's your name?" he asked the caller.

"Mr. Canaday, it wouldn't mean anything to you if I told you."

"I see. Then you aren't taking a check."

"This has got to be cash. Strictly cash."

"All right. Tell me when you'll deliver, and I'll have the money ready."

"I can't deliver. Sorry, but I haven't got the wheels, and I don't plan to borrow them. Once you and I do our business, there's no reason we should see each other again. If you want whiskey, just say so, and it'll be ready when you come for it. Only let me know now. I want to move it right away."

"Tomorrow," said Canaday.

"I'd rather do it tonight," said the caller.

Canaday explained that he didn't keep cash in the house, and, after some hesitation, the anonymous caller agreed to telephone Canaday at six the next evening.

At six the next evening, Canaday was waiting and the call came through on schedule. Canaday was instructed to bring the cash to a warehouse in the downtown area, to come alone, and to be at the warehouse within twenty minutes.

"How will I know you?" Canaday asked.

"You don't need to know me," said the man on the telephone. "I'll know you."

He hung up, and Canaday left his home driving his big station wagon. In less then twenty minutes he pulled up at the loading dock behind an abandoned warehouse at the designated location. He parked and waited, and presently a man approached the station wagon on the passenger side.

"You ready to take the shipment?" said the man. Canaday recognized the voice. He did not recognize the man, who was average size, average build, and could have been anywhere between twenty-seven and thirty-five.

Canaday looked at the warehouse. "It's in there?"

"Yeah. I've got a friend inside. He'll help load the stuff. Got the money?"

Canaday displayed a roll of bills. The man took the money from him and counted it quickly. "Right," he said. "Okay. Relax, Mr. Canaday. You don't need to sweat on this."

He turned and climbed the steps to the loading dock, leaned on one of the big doors and went into the warehouse.

He did not come out again.

After a few minutes, Canaday followed him into the warehouse. He found the place empty, except for a few broken crates and a lot of dust and cobwebs. There was no whiskey. There was no second man. There was no trace of the anonymous vendor of whiskey.

Canaday had been a chump.

Most chumps are too embarrassed to report a swindle like this. Canaday was the exception. He had been taken for $500, and he didn't like it. He spent the evening at the police department going through mug books, but he was not able to identify that very average-appearing man who had taken his cash in that alley.

THE SALE OF SUPPOSEDLY STOLEN OR SMUGGLED LIQUOR IS

LIKELY TO BE MORE PREVALENT IN COASTAL AREAS AND IN CITIES NEAR THE BORDERS OF THE UNITED STATES. THEN IT CAN BE IMPLI-ED THAT THE DUTY-FREE GROG WAS BROUGHT IN BY BOAT OR WAS SOMEHOW TRANSPORTED ACROSS THE BORDER. THE SALE OF OTH-ER TYPES OF "STOLEN" MERCHANDISE CAN OCCUR ANYWHERE IN THE COUNTRY. FOR A TIME IT WAS "HOT" TELEVISION SETS. The con men who peddled color television sets for fifty or seventy dollars often went to more trouble than the bunco artists who hawk smuggled liquor. Some of them packaged their nonpro-duct. The victim could be anyone with fifty or seventy dollars. The really ideal victim was someone with about $500 in ready cash and an elastic conscience.

John Jamison appeared to be an ideal victim. He was a televi-sion repairman with a flourishing business. He owned his own home. His car was free and clear, and he had an emergency fund in the bank. He lived in a tract outside a large city in the Midwest, and he was at home when he received a telephone call from a man who declined to identify himself, but announced that he had a bargain for Jamison. The man could offer him a big name color TV, brand new, direct from the factory, for only $100. If Jamison wanted to go for a lot of five sets, the price would be only $450 for the five.

The businessman who is not averse to dealing with crooks might think there was no way Jamison could lose on a deal like this. He knew instantly that the sets had to be stolen, but if that did not trouble him he could buy them, put them in his shop, and sell them almost at wholesale and still be ahead.

It troubled Jamison when he considered the possible conse-quences of dealing in stolen property. He did not want to be a fence. He advised his caller that he would obtain $450 in cash the following day, and would accept five of the television sets. The caller agreed to telephone Jamison at his shop the next morning and arrange for Jamison to pick up the sets.

The next morning, Jamison was waiting in his shop. Waiting with him was a detective from the bunco squad. When the tele-phone call came, Jamison was instructed to drive his panel truck to the rear of a furniture store in the downtown area.

Jamison and the bunco cop followed instructions. It was still early when they reached the furniture store, and the loading area in the rear was a bustle of activity, with vans backing in, discharging their cargoes, then pulling away again. Jamison's truck was stalled in the loading area for twenty minutes before it was approached by a young man in coveralls.

"Don't back into the loading dock," warned the young man. "The stuff's over in the side alley between the building and the fence. Pull over there."

Jamison followed directions. He pulled into the alley, and there he saw five cartons. They were real honest-to-goodness TV cartons, fresh from the factory and apparently unopened. They were partly, but not completely, concealed under a torn mattress.

The young man in coveralls attempted to open the rear doors of Jamison's panel truck. They were locked, so he walked around to the driver's side. "Wait here," he told Jamison. "I'll get a guy to help me." He glanced across at the plainclothesman sitting beside Jamison, then waded away into the loading area shouting, "Hey, Harry!"

Jamison and the detective waited, with Jamison holding a dummy roll of bills — two fives on the outside and paper padding out the rest.

The young man in coveralls did not return.

After fifteen minutes, Jamison and the detective climbed out of the panel truck and investigated those tempting, sealed boxes. The boxes did not contain television sets; they were filled with cement building blocks — enough to equal the weight of a television set.

In the Jamison case, the police couldn't act immediately even though Jamison and the detective both identified the young man in coveralls from mug books. He was a young man who was an articulate and experienced operator of bunco dodges supposedly involving stolen property. However, warned by some instinct that Jamison's companion was a policeman, he had not mentioned the television sets directly to Jamison, nor had he asked for nor received any money.

He was lucky that time.

Jamison also was lucky and wise, and not at all an "ideal victim."

There were numerous variations on the pitch used by the con artist who tried to take Jamison. Some cons who specialize in "hot" merchandise will deliver a factory carton containing junk auto parts. Some will deliver to the mark a supposedly legitimate waybill from a warehouse. The implication is, of course, that the con man knows someone employed in the warehouse who is on the take. The mark who pays cash for such a waybill need only rent a truck, drive to the warehouse, and present the waybill at the warehouse; and he will have no trouble gathering up the merchandise. In at least one case, a very helpful bunco artist assisted his victim to the extent of renting a truck for him, using forged credentials and a stolen credit card.

Some confidence men in New York zeroed in on staff members of various publishing houses. An associate editor, for example, might be approached by a man who claimed to be a friend of the president of the publishing firm. The con would offer the associate editor a combination stereo and color television set for a ridiculously low price. The con was, of course, gambling on the odds that junior members of publishing firms often do not know the president or the publisher well enough to confirm the acquaintance. The cons were convincing, and they convinced the young editors — and art directors and photographers — that they were indeed friends of the publishers. They accepted payment for the stereo-TV combinations in cash and they then disappeared without even bothering to deliver a box of rocks.

At one point, this approach was so widespread that the president of one firm sent the following memo to all of his employees:

> It has come to my attention that confidence men have been preying on employees of publishing houses and professing to be close friends of the president or publisher. This will inform all employees that none of my acquaintances sell TV sets. I have not authorized any individual to contact my employees, and I do most urgently request that all my employees buy their sets from established merchants.

In another variation on the game, the con man actually delivered a perfectly satisfactory, brand new television set to his victim. The victim, hooked and believing that the con had at his disposal any number of "hot" sets, made arrangements with a number of his friends so that they, too, could enjoy inexpensive color TV. In one case, a mark collected from his friends a total of $6,000 and handed the money over to the flim-flam man. The payment was to cover the purchase of twenty sets, which were to be waiting, loaded, on a truck near the victim's place of business. The truck was indeed parked in the proper place, but when the victim opened it to examine the twenty sets, he found it empty.

"The cons really are artists," said Lt. H. E. Netsch, of the Miami police. "Sometimes there isn't anything delivered at all, once the sucker has made his payment. Sometimes there's a box of rocks. If a box of rocks strikes a con as crude, or if there's a chance the sucker may open the box before the con can get away with the money, the con may put a piece of cardboard on top of the rocks and cover it with walnut contact paper. It looks like the top of a TV console. Or they go one step further and cover the rocks with the cardboard and contact paper, then put styrofoam packing on top of the cardboard. That really looks good."

AND, OF COURSE, IF "SMUGGLED" WHISKEY AND "STOLEN" TELEVISION SETS AREN'T GOING WELL THIS SEASON, SOMETHING ELSE WILL BE. STOLEN AIRLINE TICKETS — AND THESE REALLY WERE STOLEN — WERE CIRCULATED SO WIDELY AT ONE TIME THAT LOSSES TO AIRLINES RAN TO HUNDREDS OF THOUSANDS OF DOLLARS. The victims of the cons who peddled these stolen tickets were often people without guile and without duplicity. They had been convinced that they could get a bargain. Perhaps a man encountered a stranger in a bar. The stranger would claim to be a travel agent who had some tickets left over from an executive discount flight plan, half the regular fare. The mark who bought the ticket at the wonderful discount rate would have no idea that the ticket was stolen until he attempted the check-in for his flight, and the attendant at the check-in desk punched the number of his ticket into a comptuer. The mark would then find himself discussing the "travel agent" and the "executive discount flight plan" with supervisory airline personnel, or with a federal marshall or with a man from the bunco squad.

The airlines, to protect themselves, had to come down hard on the purchasers of stolen tickets, and sometimes it hurt. "Most of the people with stolen tickets come from a poorer section of town," said one airline official. "They are the people who can least afford to lose $100 or so on a ticket. I feel sorry for them. They're not the criminals. They think they've had a good deal buying tickets, that's all."

However sorry the officials might be, they could not allow the victims to fly because they had been taken in by a con. Employees of every airline were given procedures on how to handle hot tickets. One line offered a twenty-five-dollar reward for any clerk who detected a stolen ticket. There are now computer terminals at most check-in desks. If necessary, flights can be delayed when a stolen ticket is detected, and the purchaser of the ticket can be removed from the plane.

How were the tickets stolen in the first place?

The unofficial police attitude was that the airlines should be more careful with their equipment. Bundles of ticket blanks can be taken if a clerk can be diverted momentarily. If passenger service personnel walk away from their validators, the validators can be lifted and used on stolen tickets.

Not all cons are so subtle. At least one large batch of tickets was stolen boldly, at gunpoint.

And there is always the possibility of the embezzling employee. One airline discovered that a supervisor had a pocketful of tickets. He was selling them to late arrivals for cash, which he was keeping.

People willing to accept "stolen" merchandise may deserve what they get. There are many frauds where the bunco artist does not claim the merchandise is "hot" but where the mark is taken anyway.

THE STONEY-BROKE GAMBLER SELLS HIS "EXPENSIVE" WATCHES AT RACETRACKS OR AIRPORTS. The victim of this scammer is usually the average citizen who enjoys an occasional day at the races, or who has to go to the airport every now and then to pick up a visiting friend or relative.

Let us say the approach is made at a race track. The victim may be standing in line, waiting to put down a five-dollar bet before the seventh race. He is accosted by a well-dressed but very nervous individual who says he has had terrible trouble handicapping horses on the first races, but that he has a sure thing going in the seventh. He can recoup his losses if he can only get his hands on twenty dollars in cash. He offers the victim a fine watch, not as an outright sale, but as security for a loan. He only wants to borrow twenty dollars, and the victim can hold the watch until the race is over. The con will then meet the victim at a designated place, repay the twenty with interest, and retrieve his watch.

The victim figures he can't lose. If the gambler's horse doesn't come in first in the seventh race, he will be able to keep the watch, which looks as if it is worth many times twenty dollars. If the gambler's horse does come in, he will regain his twenty and then some.

If the victim does part with the twenty, and does accept that elegant watch as security for the loan, he will surely never see the gambler again. He will be in exactly the same position as the mark who purchases a "hot" watch from a "thief" in a supermarket parking lot.

This scheme works just as well in airports, where the victims are often approached in the parking lots, told that the scammer is just returning from Las Vegas, where he has lost his last cent, and that he doesn't have enough money to get from the airport to his home. The watch is offered as security for a loan to cover cab fare. The scammer promises to redeem the watch. Of course, he does not.

CON MEN PEDDLING WORTHLESS MERCHANDISE ARE OFTEN SLEIGHT-OF-HAND ARTISTS, AND OFTEN ENLIST THE UNWITTING AID OF LEGITIMATE EXPERTS. A good con can make an approach to a mark almost anywhere — in a restaurant, on the street, in a parking lot. Once the con has engaged his mark in conversation, he can induce the mark to believe that he is down on his luck and must sell his ring, his watch, his mother's diamond brooch, it doesn't matter what, so long as the mark believes that he is getting an unbelievable bargain.

The con and the mark may go into a jeweler's or a pawnbroker's to have the article examined. The jeweler or the pawnbroker is not an accomplice of the con man. He is a legitimate businessman. However, what he examines will be indeed a piece of jewelry or a watch which is worth far more than the con is asking (or, in the case of some watches, which is so clever an imitation that it will fool the businessman who specializes in dealing in watches). The jeweler assures the con and the mark that the article being offered for sale is the real McCoy.

The con then palms the real ring (or watch or brooch) and sells the mark a piece of jewelry consisting of copper-plated tin and set with genuine glass chips.

By the time the mark realizes that he has been taken, the con may be in another city, doing it again.

FLIM-FLAM MEN NEED NOT ALWAYS BE SLEIGHT-OF-HAND ARTISTS. THEY CAN USE A NUMBER OF METHODS TO CONVINCE A VICTIM THAT AN ALMOST WORTHLESS OBJECT REALLY HAS GREAT VALUE. A classic case, still remembered by one old-time law enforcement officer, involved a violin.

"I was a young kid then," said the cop, "working in a music store. It was a small store, just the owner and me. One day this stranger came into the store and bought some sheet music and left. A couple of days later he came in and bought some more.

"Then one day he wanted more music, but he said he didn't have enough money, but he had a violin. Could he leave the violin as a deposit for more music, and in a couple of days he'd come back and pick up the instrument? Shoot, why not? The owner said sure, even though the stranger pointed out that the violin was one of the cheapest made.

"The owner took the violin and put it on a shelf behind the counter. That afternoon, a man in a dark suit came in. He bought some books of music and paid for them with a big bill, a ten, and that was big in those days. He saw the violin and he asked to look at it. I let him handle it and he got all excited. He said it was a genuine Amati, worth hundreds of dollars. He said it needed fixing up, but it was valuable. He wanted that fiddle, and he was willing to pay three hundred dollars for it. He promised to come back the next day to see if it was for sale.

"So the guy who owned the store, he figured the customer who'd left the violin was broke, and he could buy it from him. He called him the next day, and he did buy it. He paid sixty-five bucks for it, and then he hung onto it and he waited for the guy in the dark suit to come back and pay *him* three hundred.

"Of course the guy never came back. Neither did the stranger who'd owned the fiddle in the first place. They probably took the first train out of town, after collecting the sixty-five bucks from my old boss. The fiddle? A hunk of junk, not worth ten bucks. So far as I know, it was still in the shop when my old boss died. Nobody wanted it.''

Would such a seemingly transparent ploy work today? Certainly it would.

Consider the case of the young man who worked in a gas station on the main highway right outside a western town. He saw a big, late-model car pull into the station one day. The driver, an overweight man in an expensive suit, told the young attendant to fill the gas tank and asked the way to the men's room.

While the attendant was filling the tank, the driver disappeared into the restroom behind the station and was gone for quite a long time. He reappeared, seeming most upset, and informed the young station attendant that he had lost a gemstone out of his ring while he was washing his hands. The attendant left his gas pumps and helped the customer search the floor of the restroom, but couldn't locate the gem which had fallen from the man's ring.

The customer described the gem as a ruby, said he had to be on his way, and gave the young attendant a business card with an address in a nearby city and a telephone number. "The stone's from my fraternity ring," said the customer, "and it means a lot to me. There's $200 in it for you if you can find it. Just call me collect at this number."

The young attendant, excited at the thought of $200, promised to check the wastepaper container and the grease trap in the restroom the first minute he could.

The customer who had lost the gem drove off.

Shortly — very shortly, before the young attendant could leave his gas pumps and complete a thorough search of the restroom — a dented pickup truck drove into the station. A shaggy young man in Levis climbed out of the truck, ordered two dollars worth of gasoline, and headed for the washroom.

The attendant very shortly saw the shaggy person returning from the washroom with something in his hand. "Hey, what do you make of this?" asked the shaggy one, holding out a red stone the size of a fingernail. He had, he said, spotted it in the wastepaper can.

The young attendant broke out in a sweat at the thought that this tattered stranger was holding an object worth $200, and his mind raced as he tried to think of a way to get the gemstone away from the other man. He hit upon a plausible lie. "Seems to me," he said, "that I remember old man Slyman losing the stone out of his high school ring. Not very valuable, but he asked me to keep an eye out for it."

The tattered stranger then asked where Slyman lived, offering to take the stone to him and perhaps collect a reward.

This made the young pump jockey sweat even harder. "I know him," said the pump jockey. "I'll call him."

"How much you think he'll pay?" wondered the stranger in the Levis.

"I don't know. I'll ask him."

The gas station attendant then went into the office of the station, pretended to make a telephone call, then, after figuring to a penny what his resources in ready cash were, he put down the telephone and went back to the shaggy man in Levis, who was tossing the red stone into the air and catching it again.

He informed the shaggy one that the old customer, Mr. Slyman, would pay fifty dollars for the return of the stone from his high school ring.

There was some haggling about this. The shaggy one who had actually "found" the stone in the washroom thought the stone looked more valuable, but at last he did consent to part with it for fifty, which the pump jockey borrowed from the till.

The shaggy person in Levis climbed into his pickup truck and drove off.

The pump jockey placed the crucial call to the number on the business card provided by the man who had lost the stone in the first place.

There was no such number.

There was no such person.

The business listed on the business card did not exist.

The pump jockey had paid fifty dollars for a piece of glass.

The flim-flam scheme is exactly the same as the one used so long ago to peddle a cheap violin, and it can be used with almost any sort of merchandise. All it takes is two con men, an eager victim and a formula:

The first con man loses, hocks, pledges or lends a worthless object.

A second con man convinces the dupe that this worthless object indeed has value.

The victim buys, hoping to resell the object to the first con man.

Both con men vanish.

IN ALL FRAUDS DEALING WITH "HOT" OR WORTHLESS MERCHAN-DISE, THE ONLY HOPE THE POLICE HAVE IS THAT THE VICTIMS WILL MAKE REPORTS SO THAT THEY KNOW BUNCO MEN ARE OPE-RATING IN THE AREA AND CAN STAKE OUT LIKELY PLACES OF OPER-ATION. In one case in the Southeast, a con artist was doing his thing with "hot" television sets in a parking lot near a National Guard armory. He was apprehended after he approached an off-duty police officer and offered him five television sets, "no questions asked," for $600. The off-duty officer agreed to purchase the sets, and showed up to take delivery along with a fellow officer. The two policemen were trailed by a couple of colleagues in an unmarked car, and the con man was taken into custody after he accepted a dummy roll of bills in payment for the "stolen" sets, which were crates of concrete blocks loaded onto a truck parked behind the armory.

It was an unlucky break for the peddler of the hot TV sets, and a lucky break for the off-duty cop. However, the off-duty cop who was approached by the con knew that a number of "hot" television sets which did not, in fact, exist had been peddled in the area and he knew, when he was approached, that what he was being offered was not "hot" property, but property that didn't even exist.

Not, of course, that he would have been interested in acquiring stolen television sets even if they did exist — except, perhaps, as evidence.

Chapter 17

EVEN IF IT ISN'T HOT,
THE SUCKER CAN GET TAKEN

PEOPLE willing to accept "stolen" merchandise may deserve exactly what they get. However, there are many frauds where the bunco artist plays not on the cupidity of the consumer, but upon his amiability; the net result is the same. The mark gets taken.

A Few Examples

THERE ARE SOME VERY YOUNG SALESPEOPLE OPERATING FROM COAST TO COAST. The usual time of operation is dusk, or on weekends, when householders are apt to be at home. The following pitch is typical:

"Good evening. I am on the Universal Cookie Team. I am sure you will wish to support our team by purchasing our excellent cookies. They are of top quality, and tonight we offer them one package for fifty cents or two packages for eighty cents, and if you take three packages I can let you have them for only one dollar."

This speech, which is delivered by a youngster wearing a jacket that has a vague athletic-team look, leads the customer who has opened the door to believe that if he buys cookies from the lad he will be contributing to some worthwhile organization, possibly a baseball team for underprivileged children.

The young salespersons can be peddling anything from cookies to chocolate bars.

Unless the young salesperson is a member of the Girl Scouts or the Campfire Girls, investigation will usually show that the "team" is simply a group of kids, and their aim is to sell their product at exhorbitant prices. The children who peddle these goodies have been carefully coached by their managers and will receive a small percentage of their take as salary or commission.

146

Can these "managers" be prosecuted?

Not usually. Like the peddlers of schlock watches, they may well have a license to sell from door to door. Unless it can be proved that the youngsters are being encouraged to make deliberate misstatements, the cookie salesmen and their ilk can continue to operate.

And, as anyone can see, there is no deliberate misstatement in the above-quoted sales spiel.

THE CUT-RATE WHOLESALER OFTEN OPERATES OUT OF A BOILER ROOM. "Mr. Mullins," he begins, when he telephones his intended victim, "I understand you do the buying for Civic Center Stationery. I represent the Hi-Line Wholesale Supply Company, and we've just missed out on a government bid for office supplies. We have a huge overstock of ball-point pens, steno pads and carbon on hand. We can make you a price for these that will certainly be to your advantage."

This pitch is usually made by telephone, and it is the white-collar twin of the con game where workmen put oil on the suckers roof with supplies left over from the job over on the next block. If the sucker bites and agreed to purchase from the Hi-Line Wholesale Supply Company, he will receive a gross or two of cheap ball-point pens made in Hong Kong and available everywhere for practically nothing. The carbon will be junk and the steno pads unsalable.

Can the mark bring criminal charges against the Hi-Line Company? Possibly, but it would be very tricky. There is nothing illegal per se about a boiler room operation, and there would have to be a number of marks willing to make complaints, and there would have to be a pattern of repeated misstatements. If the Hi-Line Supply Company is an entity and the mark receives his merchandise, he may have to chalk it up to experience. He was gullible, did business with someone he didn't know, and he paid too much for junk.

THE PROFESSIONAL STUDENTS CALL IN PERSON. "I'm in my second year at Backwater University, and if I get just fifteen more votes I'll have a full scholarship covering my third year. Can I ask you for your vote?"

This is a standard pitch with door-to-door vendors of magazines. The "votes" they request will take the form of subscription orders.

Are these young people putting themselves through college? In most cases, they are not. They are selling magazines.

Can they be prosecuted for fraud?

Not unless they simply depart with the customer's check, pocket the money, and are never heard from again. However, before prosecuting them, law enforcement officials would have to catch them, almost impossible to do. They move too quickly. If the subscriptions are delivered as promised, the customer may find that he has signed a bad contract, with exhorbitant payments to be made over a long period of time, but he has not actually been defrauded. He has simply paid too much for too little.

"BAIT AND SWITCH" IS A VERY OLD PLOY. "Good morning, Mrs. Jones! This is Mr. Blatt of the Harper Home Furnishings Company. I'm happy to inform you that you have been chosen today's winner of the Harper Electric Sewing Machine. When may we expect you in to collect your machine?"

This pitch is usually made by telephone. The "free" sewing machine is the "bait" which will get the sucker into the store. The "switch" occurs when the sucker finds that to obtain the machine he or she must sign a service contract equal to more than the cost of the machine. Variations on "bait and switch" are numerous. A company may advertise merchandise at such a low cost that the customer cannot resist investigating, then the customer will be shown an appliance or a piece of furniture so shoddy that it wouldn't be worth carrying home. He may then be pressured into buying an article of better quality at a highly inflated price.

Fraud? In some areas, if it can be proved that a company consistently operates in this manner, there are statutes to protect the customer and to make it possible for him to regain some of his lost money. The law enforcement officer, and consumer protection boards, should take complaints and compare. The very least they can do when a sucker calls in is to inform him that ethical businesses do not operate in this manner.

THE ADVERTISING SALESMAN MAY BE SELLING NOTHING BUT DEAD SPACE. "Mr. Smith, I'm the editor of *Nuts and Bolts*. For a very reasonable sum, you can place an ad for your delicatessen in

our magazine. I'm sure you know that Big Time Machine Parts
employees pass here every day after the shift changes at Big Time.
It will be to your advantage to make Big Time personnel aware of
your store. I happen to know — ha-ha — that a lot of them like to
pick up a six pack of beer after work. Why shouldn't they buy it
here?"

The implication is, of course, that the publications *Nuts and
Bolts* is the house organ of Big Time Machine Parts and is read by
all Big Time employees.

If the editor does indeed publish the house organ and if the
house organ does indeed read the employees of Big Time Machine
Parts, there is no fraud. The editor is just a space salesman drum-
ming up business.

If the magazine is not, in fact, the house organ, and if enough
complaints can be compiled, fraud can be proved, even if the
"editor" does indeed bring out some sort of publication and even
if the advertisement for which the businessman pays does appear
in the publication. If the publication does not reach the persons
the editor promised it would reach, the businessman has been
defrauded.

Some con men print advertisements in their "house organs"
whether the businessman orders them or not. They then bill the
businessman for the ad, and they may even dun him for money or
threaten a suit. If the law enforcement man gets wind of this sort
of operation, he may wish to contact other firms whose names
appear in advertising in the publication. Case history piled upon
case history can prove intent to defraud.

DEMONSTRATORS OFTEN TAKE AWAY MORE THAN THEY BRING.
"Mrs. Anderson, I know that you already have a hearing aid, but I
get ten dollars from my company for every demonstration I give.
Won't you let me show our product to you?"

It is elderly people, living alone or perhaps in institutions, who
are most often victimized by this sort of con. The older person,
unsure and lonely, is gratified by the attention of an engaging
younger one and can easily be talked into buying goods or services
he doesn't want or can't afford.

One case was given to the author by a very large policeman who
prefers to remain anonymous for reasons that will shortly become

apparent:

"I got a call from this woman's daughter," said the cop. "She came home from work and her mother, who was somewhere in the eighties, had had a visit from a guy who was peddling hearing aids. The old lady had a hearing aid and didn't need another, but the guy asked if he couldn't demonstrate. So she's a nice old lady and she let him do his thing. He tested her hearing or something, I don't know what exactly, and then he asked her to sign a paper. He made out like it was a statement from her that he did the demonstration so his company would pay him for it. What she really signed was a sales contract, and somehow he talked her around to giving him a check for ten dollars.

"Now, she didn't have ten to spare, and she didn't have any way of paying another $175 for a hearing aid. Her daughter had called the company and they said the order couldn't be cancelled; it was a special order and they'd already phoned in for the parts. Hell, they're all special orders!

"I went around and talked to the old lady. I couldn't get much of a straight story from her, and I could see how that guy could have conned her without busting a gut. So I told her not to open the door, ever, when her daughter wasn't home. Then I went down to that lousy company, and I told them what they could do with their lousy hearing aid. I asked for the check and the contract. The guy started to tell me to get lost, but I stepped on his lines and I told him I was going to separate him into two parts, real slow, if he didn't give me the paper.

"He gave me the contract and the check.

"I went back to the apartment and rang the doorbell. I wanted to give the old lady her check back. She opened the peephole in the front door and I could see her eyeballing me. You know what she says? She says, 'I'm sorry, but that nice policeman who was here told me not to open the door.'

"So even if I could have hung a charge on that hearing aid guy, who could go into court with that old lady as a witness?"

A large, strong cop who is willing to go to the trouble of bisecting a con man had better be careful that no one sees him doing that thing.

Perhaps not too direct and satisfying, but safer and in the long run more effective, is the action of an Assistant District Attorney who received a complaint from a woman who was a resident in a home for elderly people. A con artist had presented himself at the home and offered to test the hearing of the inmates at no charge to the home or to the patient. The people who ran the institution permitted him to do this, thinking that he was only performing a service for the patients which they might possibly need.

According to the results of the "tests" everyone in the place did need a hearing aid, and the hearing aids were delivered. Since the residents of the home were receiving state aid, the state was billed for the hearing aids.

Since the majority of the old people in that home were senile and/or deaf, the entire matter might have been quietly forgotten; and the state might have paid for those hearing aids and none the wiser.

One woman, the outraged lady who called the District Attorney's Office, was not senile and she was not deaf. She had received a hearing aid which she had not ordered, did not need, and did not want. She had no intentions of permitting *anyone* to pay for it.

The company which had attempted to defraud the state by selling overpriced hearing aids to the inmates of the home was charged with fraud.

"Most of the people in that place were in no condition to be witnesses against the cons," reported the Assistant District Attorney who prosecuted the case. "However, I was able to talk with three who were ideal witnesses — old, of course, but still sharp. They knew what was going on. And I didn't even try to bring them into court. I brought the jury out to the home, and they gave their testimony there."

It worked. It put the cons out of business.

It also made headlines in the newspapers, so that people who are charged with the care of the elderly — employees of similar homes, and also middle-aged sons and daughters with older parents living in their homes — could learn that such bunks can take place. If they were paying attention, they may prevent similar episodes in the future.

Chapter 18

CARNIVAL CONS AND THE EASY MARK

Anybody who thinks the carnival went out with the space age is living in an inner-city ivory tower. Any place there's an empty acre of ground to set up in a midway and a few rides, there are scores of "carnys" vying for the privilege of renting the real estate. Throughout the summer they sprout like mushrooms, overnight, in the small and not-so-small towns all over the United States.

Some Carnival Men Are Honest, But Some Are Not, as Wilbur Ziegler Learned — the Hard Way. Wilbur lived in a small Nebraska town, where he was something of a hero. Nobody could kick a football farther or throw a baseball faster than Wilbur. "When he reaches his full height, he'll be unstoppable," said the neighbors.

One evening the meadow at the edge of Wilbur's town was empty. The next afternoon it was full. There was Prince's Greater Dakota Shows, complete with garden of freaks, the Octopus, Rockoplane, banners and bunting and popcorn, and a key-shaped midway sided with games of chance and skill. At sundown the strings of Christmas tree lights blinked on, the Octopus started up, the nasal invitations to try your luck mixed with the recorded Sousa marches, the smell of cotton candy permeated the air, and Wilbur was ready.

He arrived with his girl on one arm and a modest entourage of hero-worshipers and townspeople trailing behind. His pitching arm was limber, his eye was keen, and his wallet was jammed with twenty-five dollars in small bills. He was ripe.

A stuffed Panda was displayed behind a baseball throw. The operator of the concession stood behind the counter and urged, "All ya gotta do is knock down three, any three, of the dolls on the rack, and the big prize is yours."

Wilbur's clique gathered around to watch him fool the out-of-towner. They all knew that nobody could throw a baseball with more speed and accuracy. Hadn't Wilbur hurled three no-hit games for the high school team last season?

He paid fifty cents for three balls, stepped two paces back from the counter, and wound up. The first ball knocked the imitation rag doll clean off the shelf. The carny man was impressed. "Looks like we got a winner here, folks. Step right over and watch him win the big prize." Wilbur threw again. The doll tipped but did not fall off the shelf. The third doll fell to the ground. Wilbur pointed to the panda. "I'll take that."

"Sorry, son, but you didn't understand. You've got to knock all three *off* the shelf. See that sign there? It explains everything. Why don't you try again?"

For knocking off two dolls, Wilbur was awarded a tiny glass beer mug.

The boy's face darkened momentarily. "All right, I'll take three more balls." This time only one doll fell off the shelf.

Five dollars later Wilbur had a collection of miniature beer glasses he didn't want, and the giant panda remained on the shelf. Try as he might, Wilbur could *not* knock all three rag doll targets off the platform.

As Wilbur began to walk away, the ball-throw operator called him back and congratulated him, shaking his hand warmly and throwing his left arm around Wilbur's shoulder. "Come back later, son, and maybe we can make a special deal for the panda."

Further down the midway was another baseball game, and Wilbur figured his luck might change. A few feet behind the counter was a board with fifty square compartments, each one barely large enough for a baseball. Each compartment had a number, and the board was on a slant so the balls bouncing from the high-number compartments at the top could easily roll into the low-number opening at the bottom.

All Wilbur had to do was hit a total of twenty points and a panda was his. The entourage gawked; with the pin-head accuracy he showed in those no-hit games, Wilbur would surely get twenty-five points, more than he needed for the big prize.

Wilbur sighted up the ball with a 5-compartment. He tossed. The ball barely missed going into a 5 and fell instead into a 2. Four more times Wilbur tossed, but the ball bounded out of the upper sections and rolled instead into the openings marked 1 and 2. His total was 15, good enough for a plaster doll but not good enough for the big prize, a stuffed bear.

Wilbur was beginning to lose his confidence, and his girl's attention was wandering. His entourage was drifting away, too.

They continued along the midway, and every operator of every game called to him, making special offers if he would patronize their establishments. Obviously Wilbur's reputation was known to these itinerant businessmen, possibly through the sport pages of the local weekly newspaper.

He tried the hoop toss. There wasn't a panda there, but his girl admitted to a liking for the gold watch Wilbur might win.

The prizes were tied to blocks of wood pointed at the top like the pyramids. The idea was to toss the hoop over the block containing the prize you wanted. The operator demonstrated, easily flipping a hoop and sliding it over a block which supported a genuine Swiss watch. He gave a handful of hoops to Wilbur.

The boy sighted and tossed, and every hoop fell clattering to the ground. Before Wilbur finished, completely frustrated, he tried for an ID bracelet with PEACE in pink plastic letters. He won, and his girl reluctantly clipped it on her wrist.

By this time Wilbur had spent most of his money. He passed a penny pitch, and the operator called to him to try his luck. Everybody certainly seemed to know about Wilbur! He tossed a few pennies, and won! First he got back a nickel and a dime and, after a few tries, a quarter. Soon a crowd gathered to watch Wilbur beat the carnival. Before he grew tired of the penny pitch, Wilbur had won back a total of $1.17!

Holding hands, he and his girl walked past the high striker. A Cub Scout in uniform was holding the huge sledge hammer; awkwardly he let it fall in the striker, and the marker shot up the thermometer-like slide and nearly rang the bell at the top. Everybody cheered. The operator twanged, "Too bad, lad, you almost won a cigar. But then, you couldn't smoke it anyway!" Everybody laughed, and the boy, flushed with pride, walked away.

Wilbur decided that this was for him. He had handled a sledge on road crews the summer before, and his shoulders were those of a bull. He'd hit the gong so hard it would ring louder than the town fire bell! He stepped forward and paid for the mallet. He hefted it. It wasn't too different from those he'd used a thousand times. He flexed his legs, straightened his back, came around with all his strength.

The marker shot upward and slid to a stop five feet from the top. The crowd oooohed, but the bell didn't ring.

Wilbur tried again. Never had he slammed a hammer down so hard. The marker rocketed upward, and stopped six feet from the bell.

The operator said, "Look, son, it's not how hard you hit it, but *how* you hit it. Look." The operator stood back and slammed the hammer onto the pad. The bell rang.

He handed the sledge back to Wilbur. Wilbur tried again. And again. Six tries later he realized he was never going to hit that gong. Whatever it took, he didn't have it.

"Wilbur, I thought you were stronger than that," his girl said. "That little kid did as good as you. What's the matter? You tired or something?"

Defeated and exhausted, Wilbur left the high striker. He started on the return trip down the midway. He passed a water tank where a clown sat on a ledge and dared Wilbur to throw a baseball and knock him into the water. Wilbur took the challenge and threw three balls at the target.

Three times the clown fell into the water.

It was satisfying but, as Wilbur's girl reminded him, "It didn't get a giant panda. How come you spent money on something that doesn't have a panda?"

Alas, there would be no panda for Wilbur; his wallet was empty. He had spent twenty-five dollars plus a small reserve, and he had nothing to show for it except a purse full of beer mugs, a plastic bracelet, and some painted bits of plaster.

Grim-faced, Wilbur and his girl left the carnival grounds.

WHAT HAPPENED TO WILBUR ZIEGLER? WHY WAS A YOUNG MAN OF HIS OBVIOUS STRENGTH, SKILL AND DETERMINATION UNABLE TO WIN A PRIZE OF ANY VALUE? To answer the question, the authors contacted a man who has spent more than thirty years working with shows, circuses and carnivals in the South and Midwest. He has operated all kinds of midway games from count stores to hanky panks. We will call him Slim.

"Wilbur was a marked man," Slim explained. "I mean it. Literally and figuratively he was marked. He had a mark on him.

"Look, a mark is a victim. In the old days, in the old-time carnys, when the agents spotted a live one, they marked his back with a piece of chalk. Then all the other agents would know that here was a sucker with an ego and, more important, with money. When the agent at the ball throw congratulated the young ballplayer, he threw his left hand around his shoulder, right? So in his left hand was a piece of soap or chalk. Wilbur was marked as a sucker. The other grifters along the midway called to him. With a few like Wilbur every night, everybody gets well.

"You've got to understand that there are more than 3,000 carnivals traveling all around the country each summer. Some are forty-milers — they stay within forty miles of home. Hell, if home is Toledo, then you've got a pretty short season. Others might have three dozen Diesel trucks and some campers, and they start out in Florida and work their way north in the spring and move back in the fall. Their season might last thirty-five or forty weeks, maybe less. Every county fair in the country has a midway. I guess carnys play nearly a hundred thousand two- or three-day stands during the season.

"Now, what I'm saying is this: Not all of these people are honest. Many are, sure. But lots aren't. And even a guy with love in his heart — mother-love and red and white and blue engraved on his soul — why, he gets a blowdown early in the season, and some wet weather, and he's not against a little gaffing to get a few extra bucks.

"But to get back to Wilbur. He never had a chance for that panda or the Swiss watch or any of the other flash. He was really up against it. Let's go into this one by one.

"*On the baseball throw, where the customer throws baseballs at dolls lined up on a shelf twenty-five or thirty feet behind the counter, there are two ways to gaff the game.*

"The shelf is always very deep, and the dolls are designed so they're broad on the bottom. Sometimes, if necessary, they are weighted. It's easy to tip one over, but the shelf is deep enough so the doll doesn't fall off. It's necessary to hit the doll very low, knocking it off its feet, so it will fall backward off the shelf.

"It takes a Vida Blue to hit the right spot with each of the three balls. And if the agent has nailed a molding — you know, a little decorative touch — to the front of the shelf, then it's impossible to knock over the dolls, even for Vida Blue.

"Now there's another way to do this. Sometimes the dolls are on a hinge, and the mark can hit any part of them to knock them over backwards. In this case the gaffer slips a small rod into place and adjusts it to keep the dolls from falling, no matter how hard they're hit."

One of the popular carnival games not available to Wilbur was throwing baseballs at milk bottles. Can't his game also be fixed?

"You bet it can — are you dumb, or something? Some of the milk bottles are wooden, weighted at the bottom. They're called 'loaders.' With the game, ladies have to knock 'em over, gents knock 'em off the table. Kids can do it when the agent stacks the loaders on top, but when the loaders are the bottom three, look out! No way!

"Or you can put them on an oval-shaped pedestal toward the front. Smacking all six of those bottles off the pedestal isn't easy. When the townie wins, the agent makes sure everybody on the midway knows about it and the big prize. What better way to get more business?

"By the way, aluminum bottles are very popular now. They make a glass-breaking sound when they're knocked around, but the gaff on them is that they're cast aluminim and the mold is made so that a seam on each side of the bottle is about 3/16th of an inch thick. The bottle simply won't roll far. A mark gets two loaders to begin, then the operator begins offering deals with odds for 'all off the table.' Again, no way."

Another of the games Wilbur couldn't master was tossing the hoop over the block of wood to which prizes are tied. Were the odds against him on this?

"The Hoop-La is one of the oldest and best. It's all in the design of the blocks. It's easy to drop a hoop from the back but not from the front. The agent, working from *behind* the hoop (and having many spare hours on rainy days to practice) can toss the hoop and win anything he wants for a demonstration. The player, working from the front, doesn't stand a snowball's chance.

"There's another way to gimmick the Hoop-La. The prize is displayed on a piece of red velvet on a 4X4. The hoop is slightly larger than the 4X4, so a clean toss can win. But the 4X4 isn't solid! It's really three thin slats of wood covered by the red velvet. After the grifter shows how easy it is, he reaches down and pushes the middle wooden slat off-center. Now it's impossible for the hoop to fall completely over the wood.

"Carny people call this 'cop and blow.' Cop is the position of the block when the operator wants to show you how easy it is to toss the ring and have it lie flat on the table. Blow is the reverse position in which there's no way of putting the ring on the block except from the rear. Many stands will flash hunting knives in front with ten or twenty dollar bills on them. The stag handle is so shaped that when faced frontward it's in the cop position — the agent wins it easily. When he retrieves the rings, he simply faces the top of the stag handle rearward and again, no way. It's blow."

And what about the high striker?

"That's one of the best crowd-pleasers in a carny. You get some skinny little kid or maybe a broad, and you let them ring the bell. And then some steel workers or gandy dancer comes along, and you put on the brake and milk him for five or ten. If he's a big spender, you give him the cigar anyway. Hell, they only cost a nickel by the gross.

"You see, the marker slides up along a track, like a railroad track, only smaller. The gaffer uses a squeeze device which pushes the two rails close together. Once he does that, nothing's going to ring that gong, no matter how hard it's hit.

"Hell, I remember reading a short story once about a mark who tried the striker. He had a confederate on a water tower with a 22. Every time he swung the hammer, his buddy fired the 22 at the gong. The agent couldn't figure out what was wrong with his brake! I laughed like hell, and I kept a sharp eye out for water towers after that, let me tell you."

The penny pitch is the game in which pennies are thrown on a board set on the ground. If the penny comes to rest on a square without touching a border or line, the player receives an amount equal to the number on the square. Naturally, there are more 1, 2, and 5 squares than there are 25 or 50. Can it be fixed?

"It's the cleanest game on the midway. No way to crook it. Toss the penny, and if it lands on the clear you pay off.

"Some people consider the game a lottery. One warning: Don't play the penny pitch for nickels. The coins are too big for a standard penny board, so the odds are in favor of the house. You can try it for dimes, but hell, I don't know anybody who's been with it more than ten minutes who'd be stupid enough to run a game like that. Not even Rockefeller would give away *that* many dimes.

"The baseball board, where the balls fall into compartments with a number, isn't very difficult to figure out.

"The compartments, cubicles, boxes, whatever you want to call them, all have numbers. It's very hard to hit a number 5. It's very easy to hit a number 1 or 2. The agent gives the chump five balls. Most of the balls roll down the board to the 1 or 2 boxes. Five balls times 2 doesn't equal 20 and a prize, no matter how you figure."

What about the Dunk the Clown, in which the customer throws a baseball at a target and if he succeeds, the clown falls into the water?

"So what about it? The clown will gladly fall in the water for half a buck. Some guys will bite the heads off chickens for less. Sometimes they'll get a local big-shot to sit over the water. The mayor or high school principal will do it. Big deal. It's hanky pank.

"Another hanky pank is the darts and balloons. No gaffs, no grift, nothing phoney. Game for the kids and the family. Get a dozen gross of slum and pass it out to the kids, and everybody'll love you."

Slum?

"Slum is any item which can be bought for a dollar a gross or less. Preferably ninety cents a gross.

"Believe it or not, there is one way you can shave the odds on winning this game. A balloon blown up full is a large target, and the rubber will break if a dart grazes it. If you don't blow up the balloon all the way — say, only half-way — the target is smaller, and the balloon will bounce away if brushed by a dart."

Wilbur Ziegler didn't visit all the games on the midway. Other games can be fixed, and Slim Turner knows them all.

"I've been in this business a long time," he said. "I started out with a model T and used the can in the filling stations. Now I own a place in Florida, and each season I go north in an air-conditioned Cadillac pulling a trailer with its own shower. I've seen lots of things change. Some of the games are the same as always: High Striker, Hoop-La, Six Cat, Fish Pond, Shooting Gallery. The carnys now have new games, too: Basketball Shoot, Football Toss, Squirt Gun Shoots. I've worked count stores (where I out-counted the rube) and alibi joints (where I explained to him that he didn't understand the rules) and hanky panks, the harmless games for the family.

"There are lots of ways to part a fool from his money. Have you ever tried to drive a nail into a log with three swipes of a hammer?

"The nails are gaffed by drawing them over a cement curbing or sidewalk, which puts a flat edge on them. So when the agent 'sets' the nail (we reserve the right to set the nail) he takes a couple of good nails from one pocket in his apron and taps them into the wood. He takes the two-way nail from another picket and sets it with the grain. When the hammer hits the gaffed nail, it seeks a sheath in the grain and follows it, eventually bending on the third or sometimes second strike. The hammer has nothing to do with the fact that the nail bends. Some people think the peen on the hammer is slanted. Not so. Hell, I've had guys come back with their own hammers to hit the nail and they still can't do it!

"Another game I've worked is the Ball and Cone.

"In this one a cone or bowling pin stands under a frame that looks like a gallows, and a ball hangs from where the noose would be. The rube swings the ball forward, aiming to tip over the cone (or pin) on the return swing.

"This is rugged enough if the framework is square. The grifter builds his frame off-center, and the job is impossible. It's a scientific fact that if the ball is pushed at an angle from the top of the bowling pin, it must come back at a reverse angle. When the agent demonstrates, his stooge leans against the framework, squaring it up. When the ball is released, it will return on its course and knock over the pin. The stooge leaves, the frame returns to off-center, and the mark can practice till the cows come home and never make it.

"On the Wheel of Fortune, the customer wins a prize every time.

"He can't lose. Right? But what does he win? A penny whistle, a pencil, a tiny bit of plastic or plaster? Slum of the worst kind.

"Every once in a while the mark wins something of value — a watch that really runs, an electric appliance that isn't too out of style, a transistor radio, a pillow with the name of his state embroidered on it.

"All wheels are basically the same, see? Most of the giveaway stuff is slum, and the flash remains and collects dust from county to county, or even from season to season. On a 150-place wheel, the standard design will have five spaces for the big come-on flash, fifteen spaces for secondary prizes, and 120 for cheap junk.

"If the operator is a grifter at heart and his wheel has little brads sticking up along the rim, he'll bend the brads outward and inward so the stoppers will slough over the big prizes.

"There are several games that are typical count-store. Two of the most common are the Fish Pond (where the customer nets a wooden fish in a tank of water — each fish has a number and some number combinations win big prizes) and the Clothes Line (the mark throws hoops at clothespins with numbers on them).

"The operator always handles the fish or the pin. He does the counting, which is why it's called a count-store. He shows you the number himself. Winning numbers 16 or 61 can be losers 91 or 19. A thumb over the top of a 7 makes it a 1. So 77 is a winner, but 11 is a loser. A good artist can make the loop of a 6 very small, so a thumb can change a 64 into a 14.

"Then there's the three-way slide. Winners are all one or two numbers, with three numbers winning slum. When the grifter nets a fish, he slides it back one space: one number, a winner; two spaces, two numbers, smaller prizes. If the mark wants to open it himself, he slides it back all three spaces and gets junk."

As Slim Turner explains, it is sometimes difficult to ascertain when a carnival is being run on the level or by grifters. Even if it is being sponsored by the local Elks or Kiwanis, or by a church, the operators may be thorough cheats. "Hell," said Slim, "we'd run gaff joints all up and down the midway and be happy to be wearing a cloak of respectability. Who's going to argue with something sponsored by the local Lutheran Church?''

And, if a crooked carnival is being sponsored by a local church or club, chances are that not only the marks, but the sponsoring organization is being taken.

There is *one* exception. Some churches and some organizations are so well established they operate their own games. In these cases, the law enforcement officer can be reasonably sure that the games are on the level. One can't picture the pastor conspiring with his committee to cheat members of his flock — or the head of an organization like the Elks coaching fellow members to gyp their neighbors. It wouldn't figure. The mind boggles.

Chapter 19

THE TALENT SCOUTS

THE scammers who exploit the hopes and ambitions of people young and old who believe they have a talent, or a new idea, can often continue to operate for long periods of time, provided they exercise care and don't actually promise too much. Once in a while a con man operating in the "talent" field will throw caution to the winds and decide to milk his victim mercilessly. If the victim screams in time and the bunco cops move fast enough, they may be able to nail the scammer.

How do th exploiters of "talent" operate? In a number of ways.

THEY CAN PROFESS, IN PRINT, THAT THEY ARE LOOKING FOR NEW RECORDING ARTISTS. Jimmie Jones was a twenty-eight-year-old Negro with a small job, big dreams, and a voice that sounded like sugared coffee. When he sang, it sounded like sugared coffee with a dollop of brandy added, and he sang whenever he got a chance. He sang at church suppers and Sunday school picnics. He strummed his ancient guitar and sang low and sweet in the mellow hours of Joey's Bar on Fifteenth Street.

Jimmie strummed and hummed, and he liked what he heard coming out of himself and his guitar. He was good. Why wasn't he in show business? All he needed was a chance. All he needed was somebody big who'd listen to him. The right ear, that was it.

The ad in the classified section of the Sunday newspaper looked like Jimmie's big chance. It wasn't a plain old one-column three-line ad. It was almost a display advertisement, two columns wide and three inches deep. The V-C Production Company was looking for new recording artists. There would be auditions all week; if you could sing, this could be your big opportunity.

Jimmie called the number given in the advertisement and was given an appointment by a receptionist who sounded as tenderly sympathetic as a young robin hatching her first eggs.

Jimmie was early for his appointment and spent fifteen minutes sitting in a reception room that looked like a photograph out of *House Beautiful,* staring at the possessor of that sweet, tenderly sympathetic voice. She was a honey blonde, with wide, blank, blue eyes.

When the buzzer sounded on the blonde's desk, she murmured a breathless, "Yes," into the telephone, and then told Jimmie that Mr. Cartwright would see him now.

The Max Factor perfection of the receptionist had somehow prepared Jimmie for the tanned, manicured, well-groomed sleekness of Mr. Victor Cartwright, owner of the V-C Production Company.

Mr. Cartwright had a desk in his office, but he wasn't barricaded behind it. Instead he lolled on a sofa, waved Jimmie to a chair, and indicated that Jimmie should go ahead and do his thing.

Jimmie caressed his old guitar, closed his eyes, imagined that he was sitting on his own front stoop in the soft summer evening, and he did his thing.

When he finished, Mr. Cartwright didn't say anything for a moment. Then he said, "I think you ought to make a tape."

Jimmie's heart leaped up. "A tape?"

"Yeah!" Mr. Cartwright looked at his watch. "I've got another audition scheduled in five mintues. I can't tell. Not from one number. You go home and make a tape. Record three songs. Can you do that by, let's see, by Friday?"

Jimmie didn't, at that moment, have the faintest idea where he could lay hands on a recording machine, but he assured Mr. Cartwright that it would be no problem. He withdrew with his guitar and took the question to Joey's Bar. As Jimmie had hoped, Joey knew where to get a recorder, for a while, and that evening Joey's regulars gathered in silent admiration as Jimmie sang his three songs for the tape recorder.

On Friday morning, Jimmie delivered his tape to the smiling, blank-eyed blonde and was told to go home and wait for Mr. Cartwright's call. The call was a week in coming, but when it came it was good.

Mr. Cartwright and his associates had listened to Jimmie's tape. The voice was good. No doubt about it, Jimmie had a future in the business. Mr. Cartwright wanted Jimmie to stop in at his earliest opportunity, say the following Monday at four, to sign a contract.

Jimmie had it made!

At four, he was staring at the contract. He read the big print, and he read the fine print, and his mouth felt dry.

"We've got to cover expenses, that's all," said Mr. Cartwright. "There isn't a cent of profit in that for V-C Productions. That's only out-of-pocket money for the recording session."

The "out-of-pocket money" amounted to $650. If Jimmie could come up with this, it would assure him five hours of studio time, the services of four musicians to back him up during the session, and the preparation of four rhythm charts. Considering union time for the musicians and for the recording technicians, it was nothing. And the contract *absolutely guaranteed* that Jimmie's recording would be heard by the heads of major recording companies.

Jimmie had $250 in the bank. That's all he had. Mr. Cartwright wasn't put out about it. He could take the $250 down and the $400 balance as soon as Jimmie could raise it — and of course, Jimmie could raise it, couldn't he?

Jimmie read all the big print and all the fine print again. It was a beautiful contract. It contained that absolute guarantee that the major record companies would hear Jimmie sing. He would raise the $400.

Jimmie signed the contract. Mr. Cartwright shook Jimmie's hand, and then gave Jimmie three new songs to learn. Jimmie's own songs were nice, but not really commercial.

Jimmie went home to learn his three new songs and to raise his $400. There was only one way to get the money. Jimmie hated to do it. It was like disowning a child, or cutting off his own legs, but Jimmie did it. He sold his car.

Three weeks later he had learned the songs perfectly. He was back at V-C Productions with a certified check. He got his receipt from the honey blonde, and he got another hearing from Mr.

Cartwright. This time Cartwright himself taped the songs, and he told Jimmie he'd have his associate — that nameless associate Jimmie never saw — listen to the tape.

Four days later Jimmie heard from Cartwright. The songs were right, but the styling needed a little work. Could Jimmie spend some time with a coach, only a few hours? It would cost fifty dollars extra, but it would save overtime on the recording session. He didn't want to run into golden time on a session with four union musicians. And Jimmie surely didn't. He pawned his watch and the gold earrings which had belonged to his mother and got the extra fifty dollars. Jimmie spent two hours with the coach, a wispy man who carped and criticized and made him very nervous, and then pronounced that Jimmie was ready.

The date was set. Jimmie would make his recording on Friday, April 23, probably at one of the studios of the XYZ Record Company. Jimmie wasn't to worry about that. Even if the facilities of the XYZ Record Company were booked solid on the 23rd, Mr. Cartwright had his own sound studio. Jimmie was to show up at ten on the Friday morning at V-C Production, and all would be well.

At ten on the Friday morning, Jimmie arrived at the offices of V-C Productions. The door stood open. Jimmie strode into the reception room and stared at the honey-blonde receptionist.

"I don't get it," said the girl.

Jimmie didn't get it, either. The reception room was empty, and so was Mr. Cartwright's office. Not a stick of that elegant furniture remained. The telephones, still connected, sat on the floors.

"I think — I think I'm having a bad dream," said the blonde.

If the girl was having a bad dream, Jimmie was having a $700 nightmare.

Jimmie took his nightmare, and his ironclad contract, to the police, who passed him along to the bunco squad.

The sergeant in bunco and frauds division scanned that beautiful ironclad contract, sighed, sat back, and began to question Jimmie. Had Mr. Cartwright mentioned any connections in the recording business? Yes, said Jimmie, he had. He said he knew a Mr. R. at the XYZ Company. He'd said Mr. R. had agreed to produce recordings if Cartwright could bring him anyone he wanted — anyone he thought had commercial possibilities. And Cartwright had assured Jimmie that his brandy-laced coffee voice was commercial. Cartwright had assured Jimmie that he'd be in with Mr. R.

The bunco detective sent Jimmie home and placed a call to Mr. R., a well-known figure in the recording industry. Mr. R. was not immediately available, and while the detective was waiting for him to call back, he had two telephone calls and three visits from other potential talents who had signed contracts, and paid money, to Mr. Cartwright, and who had just discovered the curiously empty office.

A check with the manager of the building in which Cartwright had his office revealed that the space had been rented four months before. The furniture had been moved in, and out, by a van from a furniture rental company. The receptionist, Miss Cheryl Moore, had been acquired from a temporary agency and had considered herself fortunate to have such a pleasantly permanent job. This tidbit of information came from the elevator starter in the building. A further check with Miss Moore's temporary agency turned up the information that Mr. Cartwright was one month behind in payments for Miss Moore's services, and Miss Moore herself was home having a severe headache. In spite of her headache, Miss Moore was able to sit up and give the bunco squad some information. Mr. Cartwright had been the kindest and most considerate of employers. He had never asked her to do anything so laborious as typing a letter. All she had to do was answer the telephone and keep his appointments straight.

Did she know where he lived? No, but she had often heard him make dinner dates. He had quite a busy social life. He especially liked a place on the east side — a posh, dark, intimate club named Geno's.

The telephone call from Mr. R., the recording executive, came at last. He did, in fact, know a man named Cartwright. Or was it Carson? He couldn't be sure. Met him someplace at a cocktail party. Yes, he answered the description that Jimmie and Miss Moore and the others had given of the nimble impresario of the V-C Production Company. Did Mr. R. in fact have any agreement

with this Cartwright or Carson? Had he ever suggested that
Cartwright or Carson bring talent to him?

Certainly he had not.

At this, the bunco men had their case. Cartwright, or Carson,
had made false statements to not one, but five hopeful, would-be
recording artists.

It remained only to pick up Cartwright. Habits are strong. Mr.
Cartwright liked to dine at Geno's. Two men from the bunco
squad stationed themselves a block from Geno's. They called the
restaurant and had Cartwright paged. The first time they tried
this, nothing happened. Mr. Cartwright wasn't among those
present. The second night, a waiter called Mr. Cartwright to the
telephone. One of the bunco men then advised Cartwright that he
knew where Cartwright was and announced that he was Jimmie
Jones and he was coming right over there to take Cartwright
apart, one small piece at a time.

The bunco detective did not sound like the sweet-voiced Jimmie, but Cartwright was too hurried to notice. "He split out of
that place so fast he probably didn't pick up the check," said the
detective. "We were waiting. We gathered him up and brought
him in. He never intended to make a single one of those recordings and he knew it, and we knew it, and he knew we knew it."

What about Jimmie's $700?

Too bad, but it costs money to dine at Geno's. It costs so much
that Jimmie will probably never be able to eat there.

Jimmie Jones' experience with Mr. Victor Cartwright was such
that the District Attorney had no trouble proving that Cartwright
intended to defraud Jimmie and the other singers who answered
his ad. The bunco squad is not always so lucky with the talent
scout scammers, and their variety is astounding.

THERE ARE THE MUSIC COMPANIES WHO ARE LOOKING FOR
SONGWRITERS. One case which came to the attention of the authors involved a fourteen-year-old girl who liked to write song
lyrics, and who also read movie magazines. There is no scarcity of
people who do both of these things.

In one movie magazine the girl noted an advertisement from a
music publishing company which was holding a contest for previously unpublished writers of lyrics. Contestants who had wor-

thy lyrics were invited to send them to an address in Hollywood.

The fourteen-year-old girl, whom we will call Paula, enthusiastically polished her latest effort and submitted it to the music publishing company.

Within two weeks, Paula was notified by mail that her lyric had won fourth place in the contest. Accompanying this joyful letter was a contract which Paula could sign and return, together with a remittance of $125. In return for this contract and the remittance, the publishing company would have her lyric put to music, have lead sheets made of the lyric and the music, have a demonstration record made "by a recognized artist, accompanied by a professional musician," and would provide Paula with one copy of her demo record and three copies of the lead sheets.

The publishing company would also provide Paula with information on how to have her song copyrighted.

Paula was in ecstacies, and she was dancing on the front steps of her home when her father returned from work, waving the letter and absolutely sure that her father would part with $125 so that she could have her song published.

Her father was of the opinion that a music publishing company which is onto a good thing will pay money for a lyric, and not demand money from a lyricist. It seemed to him that these folk in Hollywood had the thing backward.

He sought the advice of a friend with some experience in the field and was told that the services guaranteed if Paula signed the contract and sent the money amounted to almost nothing.

Some hack who could grind out, or swipe, tunes would noodle out a little melody to fit the lyric Paula had written.

Publication would indeed occur, and probably would take the form of a few sheets of music being placed on sale in some obscure store.

Paula would receive her lead sheets and her demo record. It does not cost a great deal to have a recording made, so long as the recording artist is not Perry Como and so long as that recording artist is not accompanied by the Boston Pops Orchestra. Hollywood is not short of people who can sing and play the piano, and who are down on their luck.

The entire cost of the music publishing company would be in

the neighborhood of about fifty or sixty dollars.

The net result, so far as Paula was concerned, would be that she could listen to her recording on her own record player, and perhaps have her lead sheets framed and hang them in her room so that she could admire them. Certainly no one else would ever see them, and her record would *not* be played on any of the local radio stations or on TV, because, having turned out the tune, the lead sheets and the demo record, the recording company would have fulfilled the terms of its contract.

They had not even offered to take the responsibility of having Paula's song protected by copyright.

Paula's father did not part with $125 so that his daughter could have a small ego trip, and Paula wrote to the publishing company and demanded the return of her lyric.

Unfortunately, the entire matter ended there. If Paula's father had chosen to take the letter and the contract from the music publishing company to the bunco squad, it might still have ended there — or perhaps it might not. The report on Paula and her lyric and her contract might have been matched with other similar reports. The bunco cops might have checked out the various complaints and found that seventy-three youngsters who submitted lyrics in that contest had all won fourth prize.

The repeating pattern that shows intent to defraud would then have been clear.

But Paula's father didn't want to get involved. He was busy and he didn't want to spend time on the case, and he was also nervous about approaching the police or the postal inspectors and being considered a crackpot. He let the whole thing drop.

Too bad. The music publishing company is still in business and still running contests. By today, the cost of getting a prize-winning lyric published is probably much more than $125, and lots of hopeful song writers are probably paying the price, and getting nothing of value.

So-called "Vanity Presses" Have Been in Operation for Years. They Live Up to the Terms of Their Contracts and Some Perform a Real Service to Their Clients. Others Are Similar to the Music Publishing Firm Described Above; They Give the Hopeful Writer Nothing of Value. The "vanity press" is one which will publish a book for a writer — for a price. The writer pays the cost of production of the book and is assured that the book will be publicized. For certain types of books — family histories to be brought out in limited editions, annals of clubs, yearbooks, and the like — there is no reason why a writer or a sponsoring organization should not pay publishing costs. "The Anderson Family in Appalachia," for example, if it is only the history of a group of related individuals named Anderson, will probably be bought only by those related individuals. Middle-America will not be that interested in the Anderson family.

The suckers who get taken by the unscrupulous operators of vanity presses are those writers who honestly and truthfully believe that what they have written is going to sell to the public. Perhaps the would-be author of a book of poems has submitted his work to all the publishing houses he knows who bring out such works and has had his poems rejected by all.

He is most discouraged.

Then he sees an advertisement in a newspaper which announces that the representative of an established publisher is in his area seeking new manuscripts. The advertisement invites all authors who have a manuscript finished, or nearly finished, to phone for an appointment. The delighted poet does so, meets an editor for the publishing house, and winds up signing a contract agreeing that the publisher will print his book, and publicize it. The cost to the writer can be several thousand dollars.

The writer's book is indeed published — nicely bound, perhaps with a photograph of the writer on the dust jacket.

The writer receives ten free copies.

Publicity is indeed given to the book, in the form of press releases mailed to periodicals which review books, none of which will review this one because the editors of such periodicals know a vanity press when they see it.

What has the writer bought?

He has seen his work in print. He probably will never see it in the local bookshop, because, while vanity presses are long on production, they are weak on distribution; and books that are not distributed, and promoted vigorously, are unlikely to attract the reading public.

Can the operator of a vanity press be accused of fraud?

Not likely. He has fulfilled the terms of his contract and given the writer his ego trip.

Actually, it would have been far cheaper for the writer to have his book printed and bound himself, and so far as literary fame is concerned, the results would have been the same.

OTHER EXPLOITERS OF TALENT INCLUDE MODEL AGENCIES WHICH DO NOT OBTAIN JOBS FOR THEIR CLIENTS, TALENT SCOUTS WITH NO CONNECTIONS, ACTOR'S AGENTS WHO ARE NOT ALLOWED INSIDE STUDIOS, AND INVENTORS' SERVICES. Inventors (or models or actors) are solicited by newspaper advertisements or personal approaches. Inventors with a new and untried gadget have been taken for thousands by organizations who claim to be able to sell the inventor's idea to a major manufacturer.

If it can be proved — again, through repeated reports taken by law enforcement officials — that the services have, in fact, done little or nothing to market the new products, charges can be brought against the services; and in some cases, if the assets of the service have not been hidden in some numbered bank account, some money may be retrieved for the swindled tinkerers.

There must be that repetition of a pattern of false and misleading statements; and if that can be compiled, the law can move in.

Model agencies and actor's agents can make a nice profit from hopeful clients who have photographs taken, by the agent's photographer, for a portfolio which the agent will show to prospective clients or to motion picture or television producers. In one case, numbers of slim, attractive young ladies each paid a modeling agent seventy-five dollars for such photographs. When they returned to the agent a week later to look at the resulting portfolio, they found that the agent had decamped.

It is quite possible that the agent's photographer did not even have film in his camera.

Most phony agents do not have to run for cover. They can string their clients along for months or even years. And it is difficult to get complaints about the agents because the clients are so hopeful, so sure that the big break will come, that someone will accept the invention, that they will get a part on television or see their faces on a magazine cover, they don't take the time to check the licensing agencies or to learn about the businesses they want to get into.

They don't know that reputable agents never charge a "fee," for example. Reputable agents work on a commission of 10 percent of the client's fee. The so-called talent agencies are a bane to all casting directors. Said one top casting man to one of the authors, "I can't help you with any scoop on them. They never come to us. They wouldn't dare. We work only with agents who are approved by the Screen Actors' Guild, and one of those fly-by-night characters wouldn't get past the front gate unless the guard was in a coma. I've never met one of those guys and I never expect to."

And those who offer to market inventions? Said one patent attorney, "I know about them. Every week, when I was on the staff of one manufacturing company, we'd get a list in from a service. That's all it was — a list of things he had available which we could market if we wanted to. We'd tear it up and throw it away. He never had anything we wanted or needed. Actually, only about 1 percent of new ideas and inventions ever reach the market."

But it is difficult to convince a would-be inventor of this as he struggles and sweats to come up with the fees the service demands. He — and the actor, the model, the dancer — are so hopeful! He has such faith in himself and his ideas. He regards a warning as an insult, and he lets himself be taken.

Only later, after long months or years of weary waiting, or after the agent or service has folded, do the complaints come in to the District Attorney or the bunco squad.

If enough complaints can be taken, if an operator of this type of bunco dodge can be brought to court, the case should be publicized. Good information is the best protection for the talented hopefuls.

Chapter 20

SOME VICTIMS HATE TO COMPLAIN

SOME victims of bunco artists would rather not set foot inside a police station. They'd rather cut their losses and forget that they've been swindled.

Who are they?

They are the ones, mostly men, who've been naughty or avaricious, and who don't want the word to get around.

THE TRAVELER IS OFTEN VICTIMIZED BY THE OPERATORS OF A GAMBLING DODGE CALLED THE COIN SMACK. It takes a pair of con men to operate the coin smack, and the usual arena of action is a bus depot or railway station, for the simple reason that people who are traveling by bus or train may have to wait to make connections, and also are going to have some real money in their wallets — nor credit cards, but cash.

The first con man approaches the victim in the waiting room of the depot, engages him in conversation, and discovers that they are headed for the same destination. The victim and the con are congenial (con men *are* congenial), and they agree to travel together. The con invites the victim to the coffee shop or perhaps the bar, to while away the time they must spend waiting for the departure of their bus or train.

In the coffee shop, the first con and the victim encounter the second con man. The first con offers to match coins to pay for the coffee, and the second con quickly offers to play odd-man for the coffee.

After having made the offer, and after the offer is accepted, the second con excuses himself and goes to the restroom.

While he is away, the first con seems to conspire with the victim. "We can take this guy," says the con. "He likes to odd-man. You hold heads and I'll hold tails, and with him odd-manning, one of us is bound to win 80 percent of the time. When we get on the bus, we can split our winnings."

Unknown to the victim, the second suspect intends to hold

174

heads the same as the victim, thus assuring that the first con will win most of the time. The victim is assured that if he loses, his money will be returned to him, as well as half of the winnings from the second con.

The second con returns from the washroom, and the men begin matching coins. Soon both the victim and the second con have lost considerable money to the first con. The second con announces that he's being cheated, shows anger, and charges off threatening to call the police.

Naturally, the victim is frightened, since the second con *has* been cheated, so far as he knows.

The first con quickly instructs the victim to beat it. "We'll split up, go separate ways, and I'll meet you on the bus," promises the con. "We'll share the dough there."

Naturally, the second con does not call the police and the first con never boards the bus.

If the victim makes a complaint at all, it is usually a report that his pocket was picked.

If the policeman taking a report on a pickpocket operating in a train station or bus depot doesn't lean too hard on the victim, the victim may admit, red-faced of course, that he has indeed been matching coins. Then the police know that a pair of bunco artists are doing their act and can be on the lookout.

There are numerous gambling cons, including very elaborate ones such as the scheme known as the Judge Baker Horse Race Swindle, where a victim is induced to bet on a sure thing. The fake bookmaking setup depicted in the film *The Sting* is a beautiful example of this type of con.

Will the victim complain?

Unlikely. Very unlikely. For one thing, he may not know he has been conned. For another, he does know he has been gambling, which is reasonably illegal in most states.

BOTH TRAVELERS AND STAY-AT-HOMES CAN BE TAKEN BY BUNCO ARTISTS WHO USE SEX AS THEIR BAIT. The most innocent of the sex bunks is the hugger-mugger. It's simple, quick, and nobody gets too tangled up.

An example:

Tom Pierson left his house on Saturday morning on his way to the hardware store. He had to pick up a new wall switch for the bathroom light. He found a parking space open in front of the store, put a nickel into the parking meter, and went into he store. He payed for his purchase with a five-dollar bill, took his change, stowed it into his wallet, put his wallet into his pocket, and returned to the street.

He did not notice the man who left the hardware store just behind him.

Once on the sidewalk, Tom Pierson encountered a young, very pretty girl who seemed to pop out of the pavement just in front of him.

"Ronnie!" she cried. She threw her arms around him and kissed him full on the mouth.

Tom Pierson did what any gentleman would have done under the circumstances. He stood still and permitted the girl to discover her mistake in her own good time.

Eventually, when she had finished kissing him, she did discover her mistake. She withdrew, blushing and fluttering.

Tom Pierson drove home, where he discovered that he did not have his wallet.

With the most gentlemanly intentions in the world, Pierson had been the victim of a hugger-mugger. That charming girl made an excellent living by rushing up to strange men on the street and embracing them. Her accomplice, a cannon or pickpocket, had followed Pierson from the hardward store, after noting the location and probably contents of his wallet, and he had removed the wallet while Tom's attention was so pleasantly engaged.

Tom Pierson did, of course, make a complaint. He described the friendly young lady, and she and her accomplice were picked up later that day while they were working in front of a supermarket on the other side of town.

But most sex bunks are never reported, for obvious reasons. The Murphy man, for example, can ply his trade in downtown hotels for long periods of time, provided he keeps moving from hotel to hotel, and provided his stock of keys holds out.

The hotel key is the Murphy man's gimmick. He has a pocket full of them, and if he is operating in, let us say, the Great Eastern

Hotel, it will be a Great Eastern key which he has in his hand.

Dick Ballantyne encountered a Murphy man in the bar of a commercial hotel in Chicago. The man walked into the bar looking as if he had nothing but time on his hands. He looked, in fact, as if he lived in the hotel — open shirt, jacket and slacks that didn't quite match. His eyes became accustomed to the light, or lack of it, and he spotted Dick, a bored businessman hunched over an ale at the far end of the bar. Dick wore the traditional garb of the white-collar traveler: a suit, subdued tie and shirt, the entire ensemble rumpled after a long day of displaying wares and haggling over contracts. He had the weary air of someone stranded away from home and wondering what to do with a long evening alone.

The Murphy man moved down the bar, took the stool next to Dick, ordered a drink and murmured, "Tough day?"

Dick Ballantyne said, "Yeah."

"And you could do with a little relaxation, right?"

"I'll say."

The Murphy man moved closer and enlarged on his theme: "Speaking of relaxation, how would you like a broad?"

"Huh?"

This was the crucial moment. A "broad" isn't in the same class with a breathless young thing who rushes up to a Tom Pierson on the street. Some traveling men like broads, and others make it a practice to steer clear of them. If this bored businessman had a Puritan streak in him, the Murphy man was out nothing except the price of a drink. However, if the victim brooding over his ale happened to be thinking of pleasant things (such as sex), the Murphy man had exactly what he needed.

"Here's a key to Room 1715," said the Murphy man. "There's a good-looking redhead up there. I mean, but stacked. Bazooms out to here. And ready for action. I'll sell you the key for twenty dollars. You go on up and open the door with the key, and she'll know what you're there for. She'll take good care of you."

Dick Ballantyne hadn't been born yesterday. He showed a streak of caution. "How come *you* get the twenty bucks? How come I don't give the money to the girl?"

"She's got a thing about asking for money," the Murphy man

explained. "She's been busted, asking for money from a vice cop."

This made a certain amount of sense. Getting busted must be an unpleasant experience. Still, Ballantyne knew better than to buy merchandise which he hadn't seen, and he hadn't quite expected to pay a double saw-buck for the evening.

"Ten dollars," he said.

The Murphy man laughed quietly. "Naw, don't get me wrong. She's not that type. Strictly high class. Eighteen."

"Fourteen."

"Naw, she wouldn't like it if she knew that I was sitting down here haggling like this."

"Sixteen."

The Murphy man relented. "Well, okay. Sixteen."

Ballantyne pulled out his wallet and handed a ten, a five, and a single to the Murphy man. In return he was handed the key to room 1715.

But the key did not open the door to room 1715. And when Ballantyne knocked at the door, no one answered.

Ballantyne immediately returned to the bar to complain. But by this time the Murphy man was at a hotel three blocks away, with the key to room 856, looking for another bored businessman.

The Murphy man is called a Murphy man probably because the first bunco artist to dream up this scheme with hotel keys was named Murphy.

The female counterpart of the Murphy man is the paddy hustler. If the paddy hustler has a key to any room at all, her victim is never going to see it. Few victims of the paddy hustler rush to call the cops, but the word gets back to bunco through the vice squad and one can reconstruct the method of operation:

A man whom we will call Harold Sweeney was staying in a reputable hotel and was having an after-dinner drink in the hotel bar, when he was approached by a woman, twenty-two to twenty-five years old, white, frosted hair, medium height and "very well built." She offered to have sex with him for an agreed-on price, which she collected then and there. She suggested her apartment-hotel in the high rent district. However, she explained that the room clerk and elevator operator knew her to be single and might cause her to be evicted if she entertained a man late in the evening.

For this reason, the suspect persuaded the victim to wait outside her hotel until she went to apartment 4G in the elevator. The victim was instructed to wait five minutes, then take the elevator to the fifth floor, find the fire stairs, and walk to the fourth floor. The suspect followed instructions and found 4G to be rented to a bank vice-president and his wife of thirty-seven years.

In another case, the victim, James (Jimmy) Conzelman, was drinking beer with a male friend in a topless bar. They made contact with a waitress in the bar. (She was dressed in a bikini, not topless.) They asked her for a date. They ordered several beers, propositioning the waitress each time. After two hours the friend went home, and the victim remained. The waitress finally agreed to engage in sexual relations with the victim, took money, and gave him the address of her apartment three miles away. The address proved to be a vacant lot.

The victim returned to the bar the next day, where the waitress who had no previous arrests or complaints, denied everything.

Three case histories (necessarily condensed) from California show remarkable similarities:

Alfred Peterson, thirty-five, and architect, picked up a girl in a bar and went to her apartment. Cash was not requested in advance. After entertaining the victim, the girl demanded money. Wallet and all ID were missing from the victim's clothing. He had no idea where he lost them.

Jose Ramierez, twenty-eight, a shipping clerk, picked up a girl in a bar. He went with her to her hotel nearby and there had sex with her. Afterwards he could not find his money to pay the girl. She punched him with her fist before he departed. He returned to the bar but was unable to find money or wallet.

Willard Crosby, fifty-two, a time-motion expert, was in a bar overlooking the ocean when he was approached by a girl offering to sell herself to him. He accepted and went with her to her apartment. They undressed, and he hung his clothing over a chair between the bed and the bathroom. Afterward the girl asked for her money, but his wallet was missing. He had only thirty-eight cents in change, which she threw at him. He offered her his watch in payment, but she threw that at him, too.

In the opinion of a California vice officer, these three sex bunks are the work of a "creeper." He explained:

"It all sounds like a creeper to me. The girl in each case was a thorough pro. She knew how to keep the guy interested and tending to business. While he's happily engaged on the bed, the creeper sneaks out of a closet or bathroom and goes through the victim's clothing. Usually the broad gets the john to put his coat and pants on a chair near the closet or toilet. Anything of value is taken from the clothes while the victim is enjoying himself, and the creeper sneaks back into hiding.

"If the broad doesn't ask for money in advance, that means she's going to take the guy for everything, not forty or fifty bucks. Usually the guy is so embarrassed he doesn't complain to us. Even if he does, there's not much we can do. Nobody can prove he didn't lose the wallet in the cab on the way to the apartment."

At that, the victim of the creeper is better off than the man who finds himself mixed up in a badger game. Ah, the badger game, a classic con. Almost every child from first grade upward has heard the term "badger game," but few people can describe it exactly. Obviously, it has nothing to do with animals, and the "bite" is never small.

The badger game isn't complicated, but it requires the services of three confidence people; it definitely requires more acting ability than that used by the dolly who kissed Tom Pierson on the street. In fact, the woman in the badger game must emote with histrionics worthy of an Academy Award. She must play the part of a neglected wife, misunderstood, put upon, and sinned against. The woman who worked the badger game on Harry Horton did everything exactly right.

The woman never worked a cocktail lounge, where the waitresses might be glacial and uncaring. She always sat at a bar where she could tell her troubles to a bartender. Listening to troubles is part of a bartender's job.

When Harry Horton entered the bar from the lobby of his hotel, he saw a trim brunette sitting morosely in front of a martini, talking to the bartender. The only empty stool at the bar was next to the brunette. Harry smiled. He was four hundred miles from home and it was going to be a long evening. Having a drink next to a trim brunette would perk things up. He sat down beside the woman and ordered a bourbon and water.

"Low, dirty, crawling snake," said the woman to the bartender.

The bartender half-listened as he poured from various bottles and dropped ice into glasses.

"Two-timing wretch!"

The bartender took some slips from the waitress and punched the totals on the cash register.

"Brutal. Can you see this eye? It was black last week, but I guess it's healed now. And I used lots of powder."

The bartender poured Johnny Walker over crushed ice.

"That tramp of a secretary. She has eight hours a day to get her slimy hooks into him. Now she's getting him nights, too. They shouldn't allow creatures like her to take shorthand. Well, I'll show him. Two can play at that game."

She faced Harry and let her eyes roam from haircut to belt line. Then she laughed, lightly and wistfully. "That bartender doesn't seem to be listening."

"Well, you could talk to me," said Harry. "I've got nobody to listen to."

She sipped her drink. "No, it's an old story. The oldest in the book."

"Try me. Sometimes I make a good audience." His drink arrived and he raised it to her before taking the first taste.

"You married?"

"Yes."

"Happily?"

"Yes. I guess so. As happily as anybody."

"You don't know how lucky you are. Do you have a secretary?"

"Yes."

"Is she pretty?"

Harry thought for a moment. "Maybe once she was. Now she's a grandmother — five times!"

"Then let me give you some advice; never get a pretty secretary." A tear slid down her left cheek. "Never, never, never!"

"I think maybe you need another drink." Harry ordered one for her and another for himself. The woman, whose name was Annette, began a long, harrowing tale about her unfaithful husband. She ended with, "But I'll pay him back — that creep, that snake, that two-timing fink."

She gazed at Harry again and took a deep breath. "How would you like to take me to dinner and then, afterwards, I mean," she giggled, "I'm not very good at this sort of thing; I've never done it before..."

Harry suggested, "You mean go to my room?"

She nodded. It was a school-girlish nod, as if she were accepting her first date. She giggled again. "Even better, we can go to my apartment. My husband's out of town, and it'll give me the greatest satisfaction to do it right on our own bed. *That*'ll show him. He's probably in bed with her in New York, and it'll be tit for tat." She giggled again at her own naughty pun.

They went to dinner at a restaurant where the woman wouldn't be recognized by her friends. They both drank more than was probably good for them. Then they went to her apartment.

Harry was beside her in bed when the door burst open, and two men rushed in. One held a 35 mm camera with a flash attachment. Before he could move, he had been recorded on film. One man stepped forward and struck the girl. "Turn my back for one minute and you're shacking up with another guy. Well, I've got you dead to rights this time. On film."

The girl stuttered, "But — but you're supposed to be in New York."

"And you're supposed to be the faithful wife, in bed with a book, not a sex fiend. Oh, this is gonna look great in court. Baby, I'm leaving you, and you won't get a dime."

The words "in court" terrified Harry Horton. He had visions of being named corespondent in a nasty trial. With pictures! There was his reputation in the company, his relationship with his wife and family. He was caught!

He began talking. He suggested that maybe this misunderstanding could be smoothed over. The irate husband suggested that for money he might consider dropping the case. Harry knew he would pay. And pay. And pay.

The badger game is one of the oldest con games, and one of the best. The beginning is usually the same, but the ending can vary. For instance:

Joseph Fortuna, fifty, a chemist, was approached in a bar by a girl who pretended to be a housewife with one child and an unfaithful husband. She gave him a sob story to get his sympathy. She ended up in his hotel room.

Two men described as "big, burly, ex-wrestler types — you know, with a big gut" broke into the room. They claimed to be private detectives and they photographed the victim and the girl in a compromising position.

The victim offered to buy off the detectives, and after deliberation they took $400 and gave him the film.

As anybody who watches TV can attest, private eyes can sometimes be bought off. Sometimes the price is high, sometimes low, depending on their reputation, their address, and whether or not they are in prime time. Not so cheap are "police detectives," as revealed in a private interview:

"Jeez, I never went through anything like it, and I hope to God I never have to again. This little chick and I got friendly at a bar in San Francisco, and she game me that song and dance about her and her husband in San Mateo with two kids, and he's running with some hot-pants widow in the neighborhood. He's spending so much time with the widow, he's leaving his wife alone. So she's in town looking for a little action.

"We go up to my room, and suddenly there's a key in the lock and these two big johns come in — God, they are big. I grab a pillow and try to hide myself, you know, when this big hood pulls out a card and says he's a member of the vice squad. The other dude is the house dick.

"House dick! You'd think in San Fran you could get by with a harmless little thing like that. But these two guys, they're not smiling. They're talking about using a public hostelry for immoral purposes or some such.

"I've got a wife and rep at home. I don't want trouble, so I offer a pay-off. We barter back and forth, and pretty soon I get them to forget what they've seen for a little over a thousand bucks.

"The two hoods leave and I look around, and the dolly has left, too. Took off like a bird. Geez, and it came on me — maybe I've been had. I asked around downstairs, and I met the house dick. Sure enough, he'd never heard of a guy looking like the one who said he was working for the hotel.

"I got to thinking about the dolly leaving, and how come they had a key to the room, and how they happened to know exactly when to be there. And do you know, I was taken! I was sucked in by the old badger game!"

As badger games go, the "private detective" is a cut-rate game. Men impersonating police officers run higher. Most expensive of all is the "offended husband." As Harry Horton unhappily learned, it costs a bundle to assuage a wounded mate's pride.

Today, with the invention of long-range photographic lenses and miniature electronic listening devices, the badger game can be more insidious and more profitable, for the con man. Today the tryst goes off as planned, and the victim has a happy evening. A week later photographs taken through a two-way mirror remind him of his fun and games. One payment isn't enough.

One victim, an insurance executive, crouched on a ledge outside the twenty-first floor of a large office building for over four hours. Fire department equipment and police were deployed. A psychiatrist was called in, and it was he who eventually talked the man into coming inside. The man admitted to an indiscretion on a business trip two weeks before. That morning, during a conference, a small package had arrived by special messenger. The package contained a tape cassette. The man played the tape after the conference and found it to be a recording of all the dialogue of the evening in question.

Considering the conservative nature of his employer and the high morals of his wife, he could see no way to survive having the tapes made public. Since he did not have the money available to make the payment demanded, he chose suicide as an alternative.

Sessions with the psychiatrist convinced the victim that his life was worth more than his reputation. He cooperated with police and identified the location of the liason. Police interviewed the girl and got a lead on the blackmailer. Though he no longer is employed by the insurance company, the man's home life was not ruined, and he has since moved with his family to another city.

As it was, he took the easy way out. Had the money been available, and had he given it to the blackmailers, he might later have been sent a second dupe tape. Letting the police handle the affair was the only solution.

There have been switches on the badger game which are also effective. One involved the young assistant manager of a hotel who watched a scantily clad guest parade through the lobby like a whore going to work. In the bar she was loud. Her proposition to a meek little salesman could be heard from wall to wall. They got on the elevator to go to his room, and she was all but undressing him. The assistant manager had enough! He wasn't going to have his hostel used as a cat house by any brazen hussy. He called the police. Together he and a vice squad officer entered the room as the woman and man were nude and intertwined. The assistant manager had them thrown into jail for immoral conduct. The following morning the woman and the salesman and their lawyer appeared at the hotel manager's desk. The hussy and the salesman were married, and they were suing the hotel for $50,000 for false arrest!

The moral to all this is that there simply isn't much moral to all this. Unless perhaps it's that you should grab for your wallet if a pretty girl rushes up to you on the street and kisses you.

Chapter 21

ALL THE LONELY LADIES

Wʜɪʟᴇ men are most frequently the victims of sex bunks, there is a variation of the badger game that can be used to wring money from women, particularly married women.

One bunco cop related to one of the authors the story of an able-bodied seaman aboard a cargo ship, who added to his income considerably by working this dodge when his ship was in port.

"The guy told me about it himself," said the cop. "I was a purser on that ship when I was younger. He worked the hotels. A lot of the women at resort hotels are bored with their old men. Either the guys are out on the golf course all the time, or they're talking shop in the bar or they fall asleep in the lobby after dinner. According to this guy, you can tell right away which dames are ready for a toss in the hay. It doesn't take long, a couple of drinks and a little conversation. If they ask, which they mostly didn't, he'd tell them he was first officer on one of the Queen of Panama liners. Why not? They wouldn't know the difference between a commodore and a wiper. So then they'd go up to the man's room and play house for a while, and then the man let the woman know he was short of cash.

"The women paid. They didn't want to, and sometimes it took them a day or two to get any hard dough out of their husbands, but they paid. If they didn't, the guy would threaten to borrow the money from their husbands.

"*That* they don't want.

"The seaman didn't hit them too hard. Depended on the kind of car the husband was driving. If it was a Ford, he'd settle for a hundred, two hundred. If it was a Caddy, it could run to a thousand. No sweat."

Tʜᴇ Nᴇɢʟᴇᴄᴛᴇᴅ Wɪғᴇ Cᴀɴ Gᴇᴛ Oғғ Cᴏᴍᴘᴀʀᴀᴛɪᴠᴇʟʏ Eᴀsɪʟʏ. Pʀᴏᴠɪᴅᴇᴅ ʜᴇʀ Hᴜsʙᴀɴᴅ Is Sᴛɪʟʟ Iɴʜᴀʟɪɴɢ ᴀɴᴅ Exʜᴀʟɪɴɢ ᴀᴛ Rᴇ-ɢᴜʟᴀʀ Iɴᴛᴇʀᴠᴀʟs, Hᴇʀ Aᴄᴄᴇss ᴛᴏ ᴛʜᴇ Rᴇᴀᴅʏ Cᴀsʜ Wɪʟʟ Bᴇ Lɪ-ᴍɪᴛᴇᴅ, ᴀɴᴅ ᴛʜᴇ Cᴏɴ Mᴀɴ Kɴᴏᴡs Tʜɪs. Hᴇ Wᴏɴ'ᴛ Pᴜsʜ Hᴇʀ

Too Hard. It's the Widows — All Those Lonely Ladies — Who Are the Targets for the Marriage Bunks. The marriage bunk does not want to play house especially, although he'll do it if it gets him where he wants to go, which is to the altar or down to the nearest justice of the peace. He's not in the badger game. He's playing for bigger stakes — everything the lonely lady has, and in the case of the middle-aged widow, that can be a considerable amount.

A widow we will call Mavis had a considerable amount. There was the insurance, of course, which her husband had arranged. There was a lump-sum settlement her husband's partners had paid after his death to buy out her interest in the business.

There was a nice house in a good neighborhood. There was the late model car, and there was a portfolio of good blue chip stocks.

And there was Mavis, alone for the first time in more than twenty years. She was unused to handling money and unhappy because the days passed without punctuation. No one left for the office in the morning and no one came home at night. There wasn't much point in cooking when there was no one to share the dinner. And Mavis wasn't invited out often. Mavis was no longer simply a friend to other women; she was possible competition, and wives of former friends didn't want her around. She was bored, lonely, frustrated, and she began to drink more than she used to.

And she took little holidays. She liked the resort hotels. They weren't too far away. She didn't have to drive for days to get to them and if they were dull she could always leave.

Besides, single men sometimes stayed at these hotels.

It was at one of the resorts that Mavis met Fred. She was sitting on the terrace reading, or pretending to read. She couldn't really see the print without her glasses, and she refused to surrender to bifocals in public.

"Damn!" said the man who was sitting over near the terrace wall, immersed in the *Wall Street Journal.*

Mavis put down her book.

"Damn!" said the man again. He scowled at Mavis.

"I beg your pardon?" said Mavis.

"Consolidated Industries went down five points," explained

the man.

"Oh," said Mavis.

"I dropped another thousand on that dog of a stock," complained the man.

"I'm sorry," said Mavis.

He grinned the grin of a true sport. "It's my own fault. I shouldn't bet on stocks, just like I shouldn't bet on horses. I always lose."

He then launched into a mildly amusing tale of a tip he had had on a sure thing. He had gone to the track, placed his bet, and the horse had had a heart attack three feet out of the starting gate.

He mused on, aloud, about how gambling is a sucker's game, whether it be on stocks or horses or roulette wheels. And who needed it? His line was plastic tubing. It was dull, he admitted, but there was almost no limit to the number of things for which people used plastic tubing, and his business almost took care of itself.

Mavis decided that plastic tubing might not be exciting; but a man with a steady income from plastic tubing, a man who had a weakness for horse races, might be kind of fun.

He was fun. He had, it seemed, been everywhere and done almost everything. When he went skiing it was in the Alps. When he went scuba diving he preferred the Caribbean. Over lunch, he told Mavis of the Pacific Islands, the dreamy land of Gauguin. Beautiful, but not in his opinion good for Americans, especially American men. If they stayed there any length of time, they tended to run to seed. Too much liquor and too many women. "Of course, I was there with my wife," he explained.

Mavis drooped.

"It was three years ago," said the man, suddenly serious. He was already calling her Mavis, and she was calling him Fred. "I'll — I'll never go back. She got sick there. It didn't look like anything at first, just a little cold. Only by the time we got back to the states, she had pneumonia. She was allergic to penicillin and..." He didn't finish the sentence, but he spread his hands, palms upward, in a gesture that told Mavis what the end had been.

"How terrible," said Mavis.

"It's weird," said Fred. "I mean, you lose the person you've lived with for so long — you don't get over it right away. There's — there's such a gap."

"I know," said Mavis, who did know. And she found herself telling Fred of her own more recent loss and the emptiness, the silent nights and the timeless days, the dragging to get up in the morning, and the reluctance to go to bed at night.

Fred understood. And where was a single person supposed to go for company? To a bar? "You know who you meet in bars," said Fred darkly.

Three weeks later, Mavis and Fred were married. It was a quiet affair, attended only by Mavis' old school friend, Betty, and Betty's husband.

Fred moved from his bachelor apartment into the house which Mavis had once shared with George.

All went as merrily as six wedding bells, although Fred was out of the house more often and for longer periods than Mavis had hoped. But the gentle social life of the middle-aged married set for which Mavis yearned did not materialize. In spite of the fact that Fred believed the manufacture of plastic tubing would take care of itself, Fred seemed troubled by his business. His fund of witty stories ran out or dried up. He was absent-minded, preoccupied. If Mavis telephoned him during the day, she could get only his secretary. At last it came out. Fred had a partner, and the partner was trouble looking for a place to happen. In fact, the trouble had found a place to happen — Fred's firm. The partner had to be bought out. He was wrecking the business.

Mavis and Fred sat down and considered ways and means. It would take a large amount of ready cash. There was George's stock portfolio. That could be liquidated, although the market wasn't at its top. Then there was Mavis' car. If she could make do for a little while without her Buick, she could use Fred's Thunderbird. And there was the house. It was almost free and clear. If they could get a mortgage on the house, a short-term loan, they could get rid of that troublesome partner. Plastic tubing was such a solid item, they'd pay off the loan in no time.

So the car went at a good price, and the bank was agreeable about the second mortgate on the house. George's stocks did reasonably well. Also there was the insurance money about which

George had been so thoughtful. Fred balked at first at taking that. Mavis insisted. George had left the money for her, to take care of her, and that's exactly wheat Fred was doing, wasn't he?

He was. He finally saw it her way. Mavis' savings account was closed out and the money deposited in Fred's checking account. Then, early one morning before Mavis was awake, Fred left. He put a note on his pillow, telling Mavis he had a breakfast appointment with the lawyer to discuss the final details of the transaction with the soon-to-be ex-partner. Fred then climbed into the Thunderbird and drove off.

It wasn't until noon that Mavis discovered her rings were missing. So was the pearl necklace which George had given her for their tenth wedding anniversary, the sterling flatware and the tea set, and George's prize collection of old coins.

When the police came to investigate the burglary, they discovered an interesting thing: there were empty closets in Mavis' house. They were the closets Fred had used. Fred's clothes were gone; so were Fred and the Thunderbird.

It took Mavis two days to realize that everything was gone: car, house, husband, bank account, everything. Mavis, the comfortable widow, was now broke, flat broke. As for the plastic tubing factory, it never was and never had been anything but an idea in Fred's fertile imagination. The "secretary" was an answering service.

After she recovered from her nervous collapse, Mavis took a job as a waitress in a fusty tearoom patronized exclusively by elderly widows who had been lucky enough not to meet anyone like Fred.

Fred eventually stumbled and fell into the hands of the law. He was careless enough to propose to a widow whose son was a lawyer who dropped in unexpectedly to visit his mother almost on the eve of the wedding. The son showed an almost pathological interest in plastic tubing. He wanted to see the factory which almost ran itself. On the way there, Fred began to sweat. He stopped for a package of cigarettes, entered a supermarket, then found a rear exit, which he used.

The widow's son was waiting at Fred's hotel when he got back there to collect his clothes. The bunco men were with him.

It was too late to do Mavis any good. Her money — the money

for which George had labored all those long years, and over which George had probably had his heart attack — was gone.

Fred ended up doing time for bigamy, and Mavis served her sentence for foolishness. She spent a long while rattling dishes in that tearoom. She hadn't taken the trouble or the thought to know the man she married. She hadn't entertained unworthy suspicions about him. Mavis had had faith, and it cost her dearly.

A LOT OF LONELY LADIES PAY THIS PRICE BECAUSE THERE ARE A LARGE NUMBER OF THEM AND THE CON MEN KNOW WHERE TO FIND THEM. THEY DO NOT HAVE TO BE MIDDLE-AGED, EITHER, OR WIDOWS OR UNATTRACTIVE. One of the authors personally encountered a stunning girl on the sunny side of twenty-five who had been taken by a marriage bunk.

"I met him in a restaurant," she related. "He was from Iran, and handsome and he seemed to have loads of money and he was terrific, really terrific. And he liked me. I could tell right away.

"So pretty soon he wanted to marry me. I don't know why I didn't marry him right away. It just seemed too quick. I wanted to wait a little, and take time to think things over.

"Meantime, he was having trouble getting cash, because all his money was in a checking account in Iran and it took so long for a check to clear. He started giving me checks, and I'd deposit them in my account. They weren't his own checks; they were signed by some friend of his. So I'd deposit the checks and then I'd write the checks for cash and give him the money. Only those checks he gave me weren't any good. Eventually they bounced, and the bank people said I'd done something called kiting.

"My father had to cover those checks so I wouldn't go to jail.

"Before the checks bounced, though, he decided I shouldn't be driving a big car because of the gas shortage. I was going out of town for a weekend, so he said he'd trade in my big car and get a Volkswagen for me. I gave him the pink slip on my car, and when I got back from my weekend I didn't have any car. I didn't have any jewelry, either. He took everything my mother had left me."

Today, that girl rides a bicycle to work, and she puts aside part of each paycheck to reimburse her father for bailing her out of a really dreadful situation.

The man? "He's still around," she reported. "I met him the

other day in a coffee shop. I talked to him, and I was pleasant. I guess that's what a con man really is — he's a guy who can take you for everything you've got, and you still can't help liking him."

Was the man prosecuted?

He was not. His name was actually not on any of those checks used to kite the girl's account. There was never any witness to discussions he and the girl had about money. There was not one scrap of evidence against him, except for the girl's word.

"Besides," said she, "it would be so sticky. I just want to forget it. I know now that the old rules really count. You shouldn't talk to strangers or lend money to men. And I guess I lucked out. I didn't marry him."

One lawyer counseled that she go to the immigration authorities and have him deported as an undesirable alien. She didn't. There was the fact that she liked him, she still liked him.

Chapter 22

THE POOR MAN'S PSYCHIATRIST
AND OTHER QUACKS

THERE are some localities where the law takes the rigid view that it is impossible to predict the future, and that it is not only impossible but criminal to predict the future for money. Fortune tellers get stomped on in these communities.

On the other hand, there are cities and towns where the authorities feel that there are worse sins than ladling out a few tidings of good things to come. The fortune teller has often been called the poor man's psychiatrist, and surely his customer feels happier knowing that he can expect a delightful surprise on the twenty-first, and that his business will prosper if he plans carefully and takes advantage of opportunities that he has been neglecting. Possibly his business *will* prosper, because he'll be keeping on watch for anything that looks like an opportunity.

ONE THING IS SURE: IF THE CLIENT KEEPS GOING TO THE FORTUNE TELLER FOR MORALE BOOSTING THE FORTUNE TELLER, LIKE THE PSYCHIATRIST, WILL SOON KNOW A GREAT DEAL ABOUT THE CLIENT. IF THE FORTUNE TELLER IS OF A LARCENOUS TURN OF MIND, HE OR SHE MAY MEET A SUCKER SO GULLIBLE THAT A "MONEY BLESSING" CAN BE PERFORMED. The money blessing, also known as "the great trick," is a scheme beloved of certain light-fingered gypsies, but it can be performed by anyone who has gained the confidence of a gullible and superstitious victim.

Let us take the case of Ramon, a dishwasher in a coffee shop in a large eastern city. Ramon was twenty-three, and a native of the Caribbean Islands, where voodoo is still practiced and where it is still much feared. Although he had lived for several years in the United States, he clung to many of the beliefs of his home island. Ramon was not happy. He was lonely. He did not like his job. He did not have enough education, or enough fluency in English, to get a better job. Also, he was heavily addicted to nicotine. He smoked cigarettes at all times when he was not actually sleeping, and he slept poorly.

He also coughed a lot.

Ramon encountered a lady who called herself Madame Zama while he was at his job in the coffee shop, smoking, and heaving racks of coffee mugs toward the dishwasher.

Madame Zama looked at him with bright interest and told him he had an interesting aura.

Ramon had no idea what an aura was, but he was glad that Madame Zama, a bright-eyed, dark-haired lady, found something about him that was of interest.

Madame Zama then asked if she could see Ramon's palm. He obliged, and realized instantly that this lady knew things — she saw things in his palm that he himself had almost forgotten. She saw the illness he had had when he was ten; or was it eleven?

He had, in fact, had measles.

She saw a love affair. It had been unhappy. It had been tragic.

Indeed, there had been a girl, a waitress in the shop, who had attracted Ramon very much, and it had been tragic. He had invited the girl to a movie, and she had stood him up.

Madame Zama also saw a terrible threat to Ramon, a weakness of the lungs.

But she saw promise, too. Perhaps the weakness could be overcome. She felt dark forces were at work, dragging Ramon down, dimming his chances, clouding his abilities. There was a possibility of better things. Could Ramon come to see her? He was a good man, that she knew. Perhaps she could help him.

Indeed Ramon could come to see her. She scribbled an address on a paper napkin and left the coffee shop, and that afternoon, as soon as he was finished with his work, Ramon changed his clothes and hurried to the address the woman had given him. It turned out to be an old apartment house, once quite elegant, but now reeking of cheap cookery and tobacco and loud with the cries of children and the shouting quarrels of their elders.

Madame Zama occupied a furnished one-room-with-kitchenette on the second floor.

That afternoon, in that dingy apartment, Madame Zama told Ramon more; she told him about his loneliness, far from the warm land where he had grown up. She saw in his palm that people turned away from him; people scorned him because of his background, of his inadequate English. They did not understand the sensitive, artistic heart which beat beneath Ramon's shabby jacket.

And, with an occasional hint from her, a half-answered question and a little nudge here and there, Ramon found himself pouring out the whole story of his life and telling her of the daily frustrations he encountered, of the scornful customers in the coffee shop who looked with unseeing eyes, even when they left tips.

Ramon got tips?

Well, but of course, The tips were pooled. All in the coffee shop shared in them. Ramon was saving his. He would go home to the islands one day, with his savings, and he would be a great man in his own place again.

Before his session with Madame Zama was over, Madame Zama knew almost to the penny what Ramon had in his savings account. She also knew what was causing him so much grief. It was that money, left by scornful, hate-filled customers. It was bad money. Cursed! He must withdraw it from the bank, bring it to her, and she would bless it, remove from it the curse which plagued Ramon, and all would be well. The future would be bright, filled with joy and success. He would indeed go home, wealthier than he had ever hoped, and would be a very big man again in his own place.

The next morning, Ramon called in to the coffee shop and reported that he could not come to work. He was ill.

He then went to the bank with his passbook, withdrew every penny of the cursed money, and carried it to Madame Zama's apartment.

Madame Zama was ready for him. She put the money on a table and produced a little cloth sack. She had Ramon himself place the money in the sack and then she sewed the sack closed, using close, careful stitches. She then drew the drapes, lit a candle, threw herself into a chair, clutched the sack of money, and appeared to go into a trance.

Ramon waited. He waited and he waited. And at last Madame Zama spoke. It was in a language Ramon didn't know, which wasn't too surprising. It was in a voice so deep and gutteral that it was not as if Madame Zama was speaking. It was as if someone or something was speaking through her.

Then the convulsions began. Madame Zama went stiff in her chair, head back, eyes rolled up into her head so that only the whites showed. She pulled herself upright, still holding fast to that money, and pitched forward onto the floor, twitching and thrashing.

Ramon wondered whether he should run for a glass of water or shout for a doctor. But then Madame Zama quieted, sighed, and opened her eyes.

She got up and thrust the sack of money into his hands.

"Go home and sleep," she advised him. "Go home and sleep with the sack under your pillow. Then come back Friday and we shall see what we shall see."

Ramon did as he was told. He went home and put the sack with the money under his pillow. But he did not sleep, or at least he did not sleep well. There was the excitement about the future. He wakened again and again, and got up again and again to pad around his room and have another cigarette, to cough, to get another glass of water.

It was nearly dawn when he reached under his pillow, touching the sack with the money in it. He felt it. It felt right. There were crisp new bills inside, and the sack was sewn shut with firm stitches. He had seen Madame Zama sew it. And yet...

And yet a terrible doubt came over Ramon. Had it looked exactly like this when she finished her work with the needle? Exactly?

Ramon began to shake. He lunged to the bureau and found a pen knife. He held the sack near the light and snipped away at those tight, secure stitches.

And he discovered that what he had was a pile of newspaper clippings.

Ramon threw on his clothes and he ran to the police station, which was only two blocks from his rooming house. He was too late. By the time the police, and Ramon, reached the faded apartment where Madame Zama resided, the lady had disappeared, taking with her Ramon's savings, nearly $800.

Madame had pulled only one version of that very old con game called the *great trick*. It is not always necessary for the fortune teller who uses this scheme to blow town. If he or she wants to stay put, the con may take a bit longer. The fortune teller has to know the pigeon very well, and there has to be a good deal of faith, which by definition is a blind belief in something which can't be proved. There is at least one case on record where a con woman removed the curse from $30,000 by pronouncing her magic spell and then burning the money (a stack of papers, of course, done up in a sack) in a ritual which involved lighted candles and a charcoal brazier. The victim, an elderly gentleman from the Orient never made a complaint. He'd been feeling poorly. Who wouldn't be feeling poorly, going around under the burden of a curse. Once the money was burned, he felt much better, thank you. His son didn't like it, and reported it, but Daddy refused to prosecute. Many victims never do prosecute. They've had their money's worth. They feel better. The poor man's psychiatrist has done well.

But what a whale of a lot of psychiatric care one could buy with $30,000!

WHEN SOMEONE SUFFERS FROM A PROLONGED AND PAINFUL ILLNESS, HE NEEDN'T BE SUPERSTITIOUS AND HE NEEDN'T CONSULT A FORTUNE TELLER TO BECOME A VICTIM. HIS LONGING FOR RELIEF WILL LEAD HIM TO TRY SOMETHING — ANYTHING — AND HE CAN BE TAKEN. THOSE WHO HAVE ARTHRITIS ARE OFTEN TAKEN IN BY PROMISES OF "MIRACLE CURES." The medical bunks aimed at the arthritis sufferer are apt to be closely tied in with the current events of the day. When uranium became a household word following the advent of the atom bomb, some victims gladly paid five or ten dollars an hour for the privilege of sitting in a dank, damp, abandoned uranium mine in the hopes that the emanation from this wonder element would help them.

Some victims paid high prices for belts stuffed with radioactive material; belts which would put an end to their misery and restore them once again to full activity. The belts turned out to be nothing more than plastic sacks filled with ordinary sand.

Victims of arthritis have paid highly to be treated with electronic machines which might turn out to be nothing more than plywood boxes, painted black and wired, with plain old electric light bulbs inside.

For a while, copper bracelets were said to be the sure-fire cure for arthritis, and thousands of them were sold.

Oddly enough, since there *is* a psychogenic factor associated with arthritis, some of the folk who sat in damp uranium mines or bought radioactive belts filled with sand *did* feel a bit better for a while, and the ones who bought copper bracelets at the least had a copper bracelet to show for their money.

How can a medical quack be recognized?

First, they often guarantee a cure. No doctor who is really a doctor and who cares even a bit about his profession and his patient will guarantee anything.

Secondly, they may claim to have a treatment which the "medical trust" or the AMA is keeping secret. The greedy members of the AMA, according to the cons, don't want people to be cured of arthiritis because they're making a fortune treating people with arthritis.

Third, the law enforcement officer who receives a complaint about a quack operating in his vicinity can check it out easily enough. He can limp into the quack's office, claim to have arthritis, and have his self-diagnosis confirmed. He can then check out the equipment and/or medication given by the quack first hand.

The law enforcement officer who does this should *not* have arthritis. If his joints ache, he should send a colleague who is pain-free.

MEDICAL BUNCO ARTISTS WHO FIND ARTHRITICS DEPRESSING CAN ALWAYS GO INTO THE WEIGHT-REDUCING BUSINESS. Some legitimate doctors are greatly interested in helping overweight people take off pounds, but there are a lot of shady operators in this field.

Since so much is up to the patient who wants to reduce, it is the doctor guaranteeing weight reduction who is suspect.

Can these wonder-workers be prosecuted?

Sometimes, but it can be a long, slow process, involving many reports, many cases and, unless a con is actually practicing medicine without a license, the participation of such bureaus as the Food and Drug Administration.

QUACKS ALSO PEDDLE TONICS, BALMS, SALVES, ELIXIRS AND APH-

RODISIACS BY MAIL. The elderly are especially vulnerable to this sort of nonsense. They can be bombarded with brochures and pamphlets extolling the virtues of pepper-uppers which will bring them a sense of well-being, instantly.

Will the tonics help? Perhaps, since many contain alcohol but a mild whiskey and soda before dinner might do as much good, and if there is something really wrong with the one who takes the tonic, that tonic might mask the symptoms and delay necessary treatment.

Will aphrodisiacs help? Only if what ailed the victim was a lack of confidence.

Can the hawkers of these pseudo-medical products be prosecuted? Certainly, they are guilty of fraud if they did, in fact, make false claims, but the authorities must know that they are operating before they can bring action. Once law enforcement officials do know, they may be able to prosecute under the mail fraud statute or bring the cons to the attention of the Food and Drug Administration.

THE MOST VICIOUS OF THE MEDICAL CONS ARE THE ONES WHO PEDDLE HOPE TO THE HOPELESS — THE CANCER QUACKS. These are the discoverers of magic formulas which will "cure" that most dreaded disease, cancer; and they are the ones who cry out most loudly against the medical profession, claiming that physicians are making a fortune on cancer and don't *want* a cure to be discovered.

"Those are the guys I'd like to get my hands on," one bunco detective said. "They say they've got some pill or injection or something and the AMA won't let them use it. So you can't get your hands on them, because most of them don't give out their stuff in the United States. The poor souls who've got cancer go to Mexico and get the treatment. Sure, they come back over the border feeling better. They come back so full of drugs they've got to feel better. Only they die. They first spend their money and then they die. Maybe some of them would live if they'd give the real doctors a chance. Lots of them are terminal, sure, and what they're buying is hope. They're a little happier for a little while, but it costs them a bundle, and they die."

Can they be prosecuted?

Not so long as they operate out of the country.

And perhaps hope isn't a bad thing to peddle to a dying person, but not if it makes a pauper of him.

Chapter 23

THERE'S SOMETHING NEW
EVERY SECOND

In the foregoing chapters, the classic bunco schemes are reviewed. However, it is impossible to cover all aspects of fraud in any one book. The confidence men have fertile imaginations, and new schemes to defraud the public are hatched every day. Before this book goes to press, dozens of variations on bunco schemes will show up in police files all over the country.

A few examples:

When the "streaking" craze swept over the United States in 1973 and people started taking off their clothes and racing around television studios and market parking lots, a comely young woman in a bar in one western state sauntered around, not too quickly, to the delight of the patrons and the bartender. While their gaze was fixed on her, two accomplices broke open the cigarette machine in the bar and departed with all the coins therein. They were apprehended some distance down the road by the state troopers. At the time they were apprehended they were accompanied by the comely young lady, who had, in the meantime, put her clothes back on.

There is, in at least one police station, a machine which was sold to a sucker who believed that it would print "real" money. There is a classic swindle, called the Greengoods swindle, where a sucker invests in a wonderful, portable printing machine that is guaranteed to turn out undetectable "counterfeit" bills — and which, in fact, turns out nothing at all. It just clicks and buzzes, or smells of strong chemicals. The machine of which the authors learned was supposed to print real money, just as authentic as that printed in Washington. It was brought into the police station by a man who purchased it for $25,000. Once he got his hands on it, he found he couldn't make it work, so he consulted the police. Perhaps they would know better how it could be made to operate.

"It's beautiful," said one of the detectives who had seen the thing. "It's got colored flashing lights and bells ring and things go buzz. Fascinating. Whoever put it together could make a fortune if he'd work on something legit. There's only one thing wrong with his contraption: It isn't good for a damned thing.

"And the guy who bought it not only had to put up $25,000, he had to practically get down on his knees and beg to be allowed to put up the $25,000. It took the con three weeks to pull it off. We'll never catch him. He beat it."

Which is, of course, what confidence men do.

So far as we have been able to ascertain, no one has bought the Brooklyn Bridge lately.

And gold bricks? For a long time everyone, even the most rural bumpkin, knew that gold wasn't peddled this way and no one bought gold bricks. As this book is being prepared, gold bullion is again a legitimate investment and the nation is in a state of financial chaos.

Has anyone sold a gold brick?

It's only a matter of time.